Frommer's®

W9-ALM-396

P O R T A B L E

Portland

4th Edition

by Karl Samson

Here's what critics say about Frommer's:

"Amazingly easy to use. Very portable, very complete."

—*Booklist*

"Detailed, accurate, and easy-to-read information for all price ranges."

—*Glamour Magazine*

WILEY

Wiley Publishing, Inc.

Published by:

WILEY PUBLISHING, INC.
111 River St.
Hoboken, NJ 07030-5774

ISBN-13: 978-0-471-78041-0
ISBN-10: 0-471-78041-3

Editor: Elizabeth Heath
Production Editor: Eric T. Schroeder
Photo Editor: Richard Fox
Cartographer: Dorit Kreisler
Production by Wiley Indianapolis Composition Services

For information on our other products and services or to obtain technical
support, please contact our Customer Care Department within the U.S. at
800/762-2974, outside the U.S. at 317/572-3993 or fax 317/572-4002.

Wiley also publishes its books in a variety of electronic formats. Some content that appears in print may not be available in electronic formats.

Manufactured in the United States of America

5 4 3 2 1

Contents

List of Maps   vi

1   The Best of Portland   1

1   The Most Unforgettable Travel Experiences 2
2   The Best Splurge Hotels 3
3   The Best Moderately Priced Hotels .4
4   The Most Unforgettable Dining Experiences 5
5   The Best Things to Do for Free (or Almost) 6
6   The Best Outdoor Activities 7
7   The Best Activities for Families 8

2   Planning Your Trip to Portland   10

1   Visitor Information 10
2   Money 10
3   When to Go 11
4   Travel Insurance, Health & Safety .15
5   Specialized Travel Resources 17
6   Planning Your Trip Online 20
7   The 21st-Century Traveler 22
    Online Traveler's Toolbox 24
8   Getting There 24

3   Getting to Know Portland   28

1   Orientation 28
    Did You Know? 32
2   Getting Around 34
    Fast Facts: Portland 38

4   Where to Stay   41

1   Downtown 44
2   Nob Hill & Northwest Portland 50
    Family-Friendly Hotels 51

3 The Rose Quarter & Irvington 52

4 Vancouver, Washington 53

5 The Airport Area & Troutdale 54

6 Westside Suburbs 56

5 Where to Dine   57

1 Downtown (Including the Skidmore
Historic District & Chinatown) 57

2 Northwest Portland (Including the Pearl District
& Nob Hill) 63

3 Southwest Portland 68

4 North & Northeast Portland 69

Family-Friendly Restaurants 69

5 Southeast Portland 70

6 Coffee, Tea, Bakeries & Pastry Shops 73

7 Quick Bites & Cheap Eats 75

6 Exploring Portland   76

1 Downtown Portland's Cultural District 77

2 Skidmore Historic District, Chinatown &
the Willamette River Waterfront 81

Pearls in the Pearl District 83

3 Washington Park & Portland's West Hills 84

Great Photo Ops 86

4 Portland's Other Public Gardens 89

The World's Smallest Park 89

5 Especially for Kids 90

6 Organized Tours 91

7 Outdoor Pursuits 93

8 Spectator Sports 97

9 Day Spas 98

7 Walking Tour of Portland   99

Walking Tour: Chinatown, Old Town & the Pearl District 99

8   Shopping   104

   1   The Shopping Scene 104
   2   Shopping A to Z 104
           The City of Books 107

9   Portland After Dark   112

   1   The Performing Arts 112
   2   The Club & Music Scene 115
   3   The Bar & Pub Scene 117
           Portland's Brewing Up a Microstorm 118
           Blend Your Own Wine 122
   4   The Gay & Lesbian Nightlife Scene 123

10   Side Trips from Portland   125

   1   The Columbia Gorge & Mount Hood Loop 125
   2   The Northern Oregon Coast 132
   3   Winery Tours 139
   4   Mount St. Helens National Volcanic Monument 144

Index   150

List of Maps

Greater Portland
   Orientation   29
Where to Stay
   in Portland   42
Where to Dine
   in Portland   58
Portland Attractions   78
Walking Tour: Chinatown,
   Old Town & the Pearl
   District   101

Portland Excursions   127
Columbia Gorge & Mount
   Hood Loop   129
The Northern Oregon
   Coast   133
Mount St. Helens National
   Volcanic Monument   145

AN INVITATION TO THE READER

In researching this book, we discovered many wonderful places—hotels, restaurants, shops, and more. We're sure you'll find others. Please tell us about them, so we can share the information with your fellow travelers in upcoming editions. If you were disappointed with a recommendation, we'd love to know that, too. Please write to:

Frommer's Portable Portland, 4th Edition
Wiley Publishing, Inc. • 111 River St. • Hoboken, NJ 07030-5774

AN ADDITIONAL NOTE

Please be advised that travel information is subject to change at any time—and this is especially true of prices. We therefore suggest that you write or call ahead for confirmation when making your travel plans. The authors, editors, and publisher cannot be held responsible for the experiences of readers while traveling. Your safety is important to us, however, so we encourage you to stay alert and be aware of your surroundings. Keep a close eye on cameras, purses, and wallets, all favorite targets of thieves and pickpockets.

ABOUT THE AUTHOR

Karl Samson lives in Oregon, where he spends his time juggling his obsessions with traveling, gardening, outdoor sports, and wine. Each winter, to dry out his webbed feet, he flees the soggy Northwest to update the *Frommer's Arizona* guide. However, he always looks forward to his return to the land of good espresso. Karl is also the author of *Frommer's Oregon,* as well as *Frommer's Washington State* and *Frommer's Seattle.*

FROMMER'S STAR RATINGS, ICONS & ABBREVIATIONS

Every hotel, restaurant, and attraction listing in this guide has been ranked for quality, value, service, amenities, and special features using a **star-rating system.** In country, state, and regional guides, we also rate towns and regions to help you narrow down your choices and budget your time accordingly. Hotels and restaurants are rated on a scale of zero (recommended) to three stars (exceptional). Attractions, shopping, nightlife, towns, and regions are rated according to the following scale: zero stars (recommended), one star (highly recommended), two stars (very highly recommended), and three stars (must-see).

In addition to the star-rating system, we also use **seven feature icons** that point you to the great deals, in-the-know advice, and unique experiences that separate travelers from tourists. Throughout the book, look for:

Finds	Special finds—those places only insiders know about
Fun Fact	Fun facts—details that make travelers more informed and their trips more fun
Kids	Best bets for kids and advice for the whole family
Moments	Special moments—those experiences that memories are made of
Overrated	Places or experiences not worth your time or money
Tips	Insider tips—great ways to save time and money
Value	Great values—where to get the best deals

The following **abbreviations** are used for credit cards:

| AE | American Express | DISC | Discover | V | Visa |
| DC | Diners Club | MC | MasterCard | | |

FROMMERS.COM

Now that you have the guidebook to a great trip, visit our website at **www.frommers.com** for travel information on more than 3,000 destinations. With features updated regularly, we give you instant access to the most current trip-planning information available. At Frommers.com, you'll also find the best prices on airfares, accommodations, and car rentals—and you can even book travel online through our travel booking partners. At Frommers.com, you'll also find the following:

- Online updates to our most popular guidebooks
- Vacation sweepstakes and contest giveaways
- Newsletter highlighting the hottest travel trends
- Online travel message boards with featured travel discussions

The Best of Portland

Situated at the confluence of the Willamette and Columbia rivers, Portland, Oregon, with a population of roughly two million in the metropolitan area, is a city of discreet charms. That the city claims a rose garden as one of its biggest attractions should give you an idea of just how laid-back this city is. Sure, Portlanders are just as attached to their cellphones and PDAs as residents of other major metropolitan areas, but this is the City of Roses, and people still take the time to stop and smell the flowers. Spend much time here, and you, too, will likely feel the city's leisurely pace seeping into your bones.

While nearby Seattle, Washington, has zoomed into the national consciousness, Portland has, until recently, managed to dodge the limelight and the problems that come with skyrocketing popularity. For many years now, Portland has looked upon itself as a small, accessible city, vaguely European in character. *Clean* and *friendly* are the two terms that crop up most often in descriptions of the city. However, as word has spread about overcrowding in Seattle, people looking for the good life and affordable housing have turned to Portland, which is now experiencing the same sort of rapid growth that Seattle began going through more than a decade ago.

Portland does not have any major tourist sights. Instead, it is a city of quiet charms that must be searched for and savored—the shade of the stately elms in the South Park Blocks, the tranquillity of the Japanese Garden, the view from the grounds of Pittock Mansion, the miles of hiking trails in Forest Park. Sure, there's a good art museum and a world-class science museum, but these are not nearly as important to the city's citizenry as the many parks and public gardens. Not only does Portland claim beautiful rose gardens, the most authentic Japanese garden in North America, and the largest classical Chinese garden in the country, but it also can lay claim to both the world's smallest city park and the largest forested urban park in the country.

The city's other claim to fame is as the nation's microbrew capital. Espresso may be the beverage that gets this town going in the morning, but it is microbrewed beer that helps the city maintain its mellow character. There are so many brewpubs here in Portland that the city has been nicknamed Munich on the Willamette. Wine bars are also popular hangouts, which shouldn't come as a surprise, considering how close the city is to the Willamette Valley wine country.

Portland itself may be short on things for visitors to do, but the city's surroundings certainly are not. Within a 1½- to 2-hour drive from Portland, you can be strolling a Pacific Ocean beach, walking beside a waterfall in the Columbia Gorge, hiking on Mount Hood (a dormant volcano as picture-perfect as Mt. Fuji), driving through the Mount St. Helens blast zone, or sampling world-class pinot noirs in the Oregon wine country. It is this proximity to the outdoors that makes Portland a great city to use as a base for exploring some of the best of the Northwest.

1 The Most Unforgettable Travel Experiences

- **Strolling the Grounds of the Japanese Garden:** This is the best Japanese garden in the United States, perhaps the best anywhere outside of Japan. My favorite time to visit is in June when the Japanese irises are in bloom. There's no better stress-reducer in the city. See p. 87.
- **Beer Sampling at Brewpubs:** They may not have invented beer here in Portland, but they certainly have turned it into an art form. Whether you're looking for a cozy corner pub or an upscale taproom, you'll find a brewpub where you can feel comfortable sampling local brewmeisters' concoctions. See "Brewpubs" in chapter 9.
- **Driving and Hiking in the Gorge:** No matter what time of year, the drive up the Columbia Gorge is spectacular, and there are dozens of easily accessible hiking trails throughout the gorge. If you've got time to spare, take the scenic highway; if not, take I-84. On either route, be sure to pull off at Multnomah Falls. For an alternative point of view, drive the Washington side of the river and stop to hike to the top of Beacon Rock. See section 1 of chapter 10, "Side Trips from Portland."
- **Concerts at the Schnitz:** The Arlene Schnitzer Concert Hall, home to the Oregon Symphony, is a restored 1920s movie palace and is the city's most impressive place to attend a performance. Even if the show doesn't meet your expectations, you can enjoy the classic architectural details. See p. 112.

- **Summertime Concerts at the Oregon Zoo:** Summertime in Portland means partying with the pachyderms. Throughout the summer, you can catch live music at the zoo's amphitheater. Musical styles include blues, rock, bluegrass, folk, Celtic, and jazz. Often, for just the price of zoo admission, you can catch the concert and tour the zoo (if you arrive early enough). Picnics are encouraged, but no alcohol is allowed into the zoo (however, beer and wine are on sale during concerts). See p. 114.
- **Summer Festivals at Waterfront Park:** Each summer, Tom McCall Waterfront Park, which stretches along the Willamette River in downtown Portland, becomes the staging ground for everything from Rose Festival events to the Oregon Brewers Festival. Some festivals are free and some have small cover charges, but all are lots of fun. See p. 81.
- **Wine Tasting in the Nearby Wine Country:** Within less than an hour's drive of Portland there are dozens of wineries that are open to the public on a regular basis. Most of these wineries specialize in pinot noir and pinot gris, and many produce wines of superior quality. The chance to spend an afternoon wine tasting is one of the best reasons to visit Portland. See p. 139.

2 The Best Splurge Hotels

- **Avalon Hotel & Spa** (0455 SW Hamilton Court; ✆ 888/556-4402 or 503/802-5800): Located just south of downtown Portland, along a wooded section of the Willamette River waterfront, the Avalon is not only one of the most luxurious hotels in the city, but it also has its own spa and boasts stylishly modern decor. See p. 44.
- **The Benson** (309 SW Broadway; ✆ 888/523-6766 or 503/228-2000): With its walnut paneling, Italian marble, and crystal chandeliers, The Benson is the pinnacle of 19th-century elegance. Order a snifter of brandy, sink into one of the leather chairs by the fireplace, and conjure up your past life as a railroad baron. In your room, you'll sleep on a Tempur-Pedic bed. See p. 48.
- **5th Avenue Suites Hotel** (506 SW Washington St.; ✆ 888/207-2201 or 503/222-0001): With a delightfully theatrical room decor, a good restaurant, a day spa, free evening wine, and an artistic aesthetic, this hotel has everything necessary to make a visit to Portland unforgettable. See p. 45.

- **Hotel Vintage Plaza** (422 SW Broadway; ✆ **800/243-0555** or 503/228-1212): If you're looking for the most romantic room in town, book a starlight room at the Vintage Plaza. Located on one of the hotel's upper floors, these romantic rooms are basically solariums with curving walls of glass that let you lie in bed and gaze up at the stars. Just be sure to come in the summer when there aren't as many clouds in the sky. See p. 46.
- **RiverPlace Hotel** (1510 SW Harbor Way; ✆ **800/227-1333** or 503/228-3233): Although it's only a few blocks from downtown businesses, this boutique hotel wedged between the Willamette River and Tom McCall Riverfront Park feels a world away from the city. In summer the park hosts countless festivals, and if you book the right room, you can have a box seat for a concert in the park. See p. 47.

3 The Best Moderately Priced Hotels

- **Four Points by Sheraton Portland Downtown** (50 SW Morrison; ✆ **800/368-7764** or 503/221-0711): Although it is totally unassuming from the outside, the Four Points, with its contemporary interior decor, is a surprisingly stylish and economically priced hotel. Waterfront Park and the Willamette River are just across the street, so you've got a great deal (if you can reserve far enough in advance to get a low rate). See p. 49.
- **Homewood Suites by Hilton Vancouver/Portland** (701 SE Columbia Shores Blvd., Vancouver; ✆ **800/CALL-HOME** or 360/750-1100): Although it is located in Vancouver, Washington, 20 minutes from downtown Portland, this hotel is a good bet for families. Guest rooms are more like apartments, and rates include breakfast and a big spread of evening appetizers. There's also a 5-mile-long paved riverside trail across the street. See p. 54.
- **Inn @ Northrup Station** (2025 NW Northrup St.; ✆ **800/224-1180** or 503/224-0543): If you're short on cash but want to stay someplace that reflects your taste for contemporary styling, then the Inn @ Northrup Station should be your first choice in town. Not only is this place cool and colorful, but there are great restaurants and bars within just a few blocks. See p. 50.
- **Jupiter Hotel** (800 E. Burnside St.; ✆ **877/800-0004** or 503/230-9200): This renovated motel in inner southeast Portland is the new hotel of choice for cash-strapped art-school

hipsters when they come to Portland to check out the nightlife scene. To make the scene at one of the city's hippest night-club's, hotel guests need only walk across the courtyard to the Doug Fir Lounge. See p. 53.

- **The Lakeshore Inn** (210 N. State St., Lake Oswego; © **800/ 215-6431** or 503/636-9679): How about a waterfront motel in Portland's most prestigious suburb for under $80? Try the Lakeshore Inn, a small motel right on Lake Oswego with a swimming pool on a dock. The catch is that the hotel is 7 miles from downtown Portland. See p. 56.

- **McMenamins Edgefield** (2126 SW Halsey St., Troutdale; © **800/669-8610** or 503/669-8610): What can you say about a hotel that's located in a renovated poor farm and has a brew-ery, winery, distillery, movie theater, and golf course? Cheers! At McMenamins Edgefield, on the eastern edge of the Port-land metro area, a local brewpub empire has created one of the most unusual lodgings in the state. See p. 55. The affiliated **McMenamins Kennedy School,** 5736 NE 33rd Ave. (© **888/ 249-3983** or 503/249-3983), is very similar and closer to downtown Portland. See p. 53.

4 The Most Unforgettable Dining Experiences

- **Bijou Café** (132 SW Third Ave.; © **503/222-3187**): Organic coffee, eggs from free-range chickens, buckwheat pancakes, oyster hash, and brioche French toast are the sort of menu offerings that have made this downtown breakfast place a perennial favorite of Portlanders. See p. 63.

- **Bluehour** (250 NW 13th Ave.; © **503/226-3394**): This utterly stylish restaurant is one of the linchpins of the trendy Pearl District, the sort of place locals frequent in order to see and be seen. The menu includes such staples as caviar and foie gras but also delves into far more creative fare. See p. 63.

- **Caprial's Bistro and Wine** (7015 SE Milwaukie Ave.; © **503/ 236-6457**): There aren't a lot of neighborhood restaurants that can boast of having a celebrity chef in the kitchen, but at Cap-rial's, in the Sellwood neighborhood of southeast Portland, you just might recognize chef Caprial Pence from TV shows and cookbooks. See p. 70.

- **Chart House** (5700 SW Terwilliger Blvd.; © **503/246-6963**): The Chart House may be part of an upscale restaurant chain, but the view from the hillside setting south of downtown Portland just can't be beat. Down at the foot of the hill is the Willamette River, and off over the rooftops and treetops of Portland are Mount Hood and Mount St. Helens. See p. 68.

- **Higgins** (1239 SW Broadway; © 503/222-9070): Chef Greg Higgins pushes the envelope of contemporary cuisine here at his eponymously named restaurant, but he also sprinkles the menu with plenty of familiar comfort foods. Sample some of Portland's best food in the formal dining room or in the casual back-room bar area. See p. 60.

- **Huber's** (411 SW Third Ave.; © 503/228-5686): This is the oldest restaurant in Portland, and whether it's Thanksgiving or not, this place specializes in turkey dinners. It also specializes in Spanish coffee, a potent liquor-laced pick-me-up. Be sure to get a table in the old room with the stained-glass ceiling. See p. 61.

- **Jake's Famous Crawfish** (401 SW 12th Ave.; © 503/226-1419): Get 'em while they're hot at Jake's, where crawfish are the stars of the menu. This classic seafood restaurant has been around for almost a century and serves truckloads of crawfish every year. There are plenty of other good seafood dishes on the menu as well. See p. 61.

- **Newport Bay Restaurant** (0425 SW Montgomery St.; © 503/227-3474): The food at this restaurant may not be superlative, but the setting—floating in the Willamette River—certainly is. Walk down the long dock, take a seat on the patio, and have a front-row seat for the comings and goings of boats on the river. See p. 62.

5 The Best Things to Do for Free (or Almost)

- **Sunset from Council Crest:** Portland is a city backed by hills that reach 1,000 feet high, and the view from atop Council Crest is the finest in the city. From here you can see mounts Rainier, St. Helens, Adams, and Hood. The view is particularly memorable at sunset. Bring a picnic.

- **Hanging Out at Powell's:** They don't call Powell's the City of Books for nothing. This bookstore, which sells both new and used books, is so big you have to get a map at the front door. No matter how much time I spend here, it's never enough. A large cafe makes it easy to while away the hours. See p. 107.

- **Free Rides on the Vintage Trolleys:** Tri-Met buses, MAX light-rail trolleys, and the Portland Streetcar are all free within a large downtown area known as the Fareless Square. That alone should be enough to get you on some form of public transit while you're in town, but if you're really lucky, you might catch one of the vintage trolley cars. There aren't any San Francisco–style hills, but these old trolley cars are still fun to ride. See p. 34.

- **People-Watching at Pioneer Courthouse Square:** This is the heart and soul of downtown Portland, and no matter what time of year or what the weather, people gather here. Grab a latte at the Starbucks and sit by the waterfall fountain. In summer there are frequent concerts here, and any time of year you might catch a rally, performance, or installation of some kind. Don't miss the *Weather Machine* show at noon. See chapter 6.

- **An Afternoon at the Portland Saturday Market:** This large arts-and-crafts market is an outdoor showcase for hundreds of the Northwest's creative artisans. You'll find fascinating one-of-a-kind clothes, jewelry, kitchenwares, musical instruments, and much, much more. The food stalls serve great fast food, too. See p. 110.

- **First Thursday Art Walk:** On the first Thursday of every month, Portland goes on an art binge. People get dressed up and go gallery-hopping from art opening to art opening. There are usually hors d'oeuvres and wine available, and sometimes there's even live music. The galleries stay open until 9pm. See p. 105.

- **Stopping to Smell the Roses:** Portland is known as the City of Roses, and at the International Rose Test Garden in Washington Park, you can find out why. This is a test garden for new varieties of roses, so you'll probably have to wait a few years before you can buy your favorite rose plant here. See p. 86.

6 The Best Outdoor Activities

- **Kayaking Around Ross Island:** Seattle may be considered the sea-kayaking capital of the Northwest, but Portland's not a bad kayaking spot itself. You can paddle on the Columbia or Willamette river, but my favorite easy paddle is around Ross Island in the Willamette River. You can even paddle past the submarine at the Oregon Museum of Science and Industry and pull out at Tom McCall Waterfront Park. See p. 95.

- **Mountain Biking Leif Erikson Drive:** Forest Park is the largest forested city park in the country, and running its length is the unpaved Leif Erikson Road. The road is closed to cars and extends for 12 miles. Along the way, there are occasional views of the Columbia River. This is a fairly easy ride, without any strenuous climbs. See p. 93.

- **Hiking Forest Park's Wildwood Trail:** Forest Park is the largest wooded urban park in the country, and within its boundaries, there are nearly 75 miles of hiking trails. The Wildwood Trail stretches for nearly 30 miles, from one end of the park to the other, and while you probably won't have time to hike the entire trail, there are lots of shorter loops possible. See p. 95.

- **Hiking and Skiing on Mount Hood:** Less than an hour from Portland, Mount Hood offers year-round skiing and hiking. Timberline Lodge, high on this dormant volcano's slopes, was built by the WPA during the Great Depression and is a show-case of craftsmanship. See section 1 of chapter 10, "Side Trips from Portland."

- **Picnicking at the Washington Park Arboretum:** Picnicking may not be a particularly strenuous outdoor activity, but an alfresco meal on a grassy hillside surrounded by rare and unusual trees sure is memorable. Before your picnic, you can work up an appetite by hiking some of the arboretum's 12 miles of trails. See p. 84.

7 The Best Activities for Families

- **Going Below Decks in a Real Submarine:** At the Oregon Museum of Science and Industry (OMSI), you can poke around inside the USS *Blueback,* a retired Navy submarine that was used in the filming of *The Hunt for Red October.* The sub is now permanently docked in the Willamette River outside the museum's back door. See p. 82.

- **Virtual Parachuting:** At the World Forestry Center Discovery Museum, you and the kids can pretend to be smoke jumpers parachuting into the woods to put out a forest fire. The virtual parachute exhibit lets you strap into a harness and try to hit a video target on the floor. See p. 88.

- **Flying Over the Water:** Giant jet boats roar up the Willamette River from the Oregon Museum of Science and Industry to the thundering cascades of Willamette Falls in Oregon City. Along the way, you'll get a unique perspective on Portland life. See p. 91.

- **Roller Skating at Oaks Park:** At the quaintly old-fashioned Oaks Park Amusement Center, you can roller skate to the accompaniment of a Wurlitzer organ. The skating rink here is the largest wood-floored rink in the West. There are also plenty of thrill rides and arcades See p. 90.
- **Riding the Rails in Washington Park:** At the Oregon Zoo, you can not only ponder the pachyderms and gaze at grizzlies, you can go for a ride on a scaled-down train that runs between the zoo and the International Rose Test Garden and the Japanese Garden. Near the end of the line with the gardens, you'll also find the Rose Garden Children's Park, a big, colorful playground. See p. 87.

2

Planning Your Trip to Portland

One of your first considerations when planning your trip should be when to visit. Summer is the peak season in the Northwest, the season for sunshine and outdoor festivals and events. During the summer months, hotel and car reservations are almost essential; the rest of the year they're highly advisable but not nearly as imperative. Keep in mind, however, that when booking a plane, hotel, or rental car, you can usually get better rates by reserving weeks in advance.

1 Visitor Information

For information on Portland and the rest of Oregon, contact the **Portland Oregon Visitors Association (POVA),** 1000 SW Broadway, Suite 2300, Portland, OR 97205 (© **877/678-5263** or 503/275-8355; www.travelportland.com).

If you're surfing the Net, you can get additional Portland information at the following websites: *Willamette Week* (**www.wweek.com**), Portland's arts-and-entertainment weekly, or the *Oregonian* (**www.oregonlive.com**), Portland's daily newspaper.

2 Money

ATMs

The easiest and best way to get cash away from home is from an ATM (automated teller machine). The **Cirrus** (© **800/424-7787;** www.mastercard.com) and **PLUS** (© **800/843-7587;** www.visa.com) networks span the globe; look at the back of your bank card to see which network you're on, then call or check online for ATM locations at your destination. Be sure you know your personal identification number (PIN) and daily withdrawal limit before you depart. *Note:* Remember that many banks impose a fee every time you use a card at another bank's ATM. In addition, the bank from which you withdraw cash may charge its own fee. To compare banks' ATM fees within the U.S., use **www.bankrate.com**.

You can use your credit card to receive cash advances at ATMs. Keep in mind that credit card companies protect themselves from theft by limiting maximum withdrawals outside their home country, so call your credit card company before you leave home. And keep in mind that you'll pay interest from the moment of your withdrawal.

TRAVELER'S CHECKS

Traveler's checks are something of an anachronism from the days before the ATM made cash accessible at any time. Given the fees you'll pay for ATM use at banks other than your own, however, you might be better off with traveler's checks if you're withdrawing money often.

You can get traveler's checks at almost any bank. **American Express** offers denominations of $20, $50, $100, $500, and (for cardholders only) $1,000. You'll pay a service charge ranging from 1% to 4%. You can also get American Express traveler's checks over the phone by calling ✆ **800/221-7282;** Amex gold and platinum cardholders who use this number are exempt from the 1% fee.

Visa offers traveler's checks at Citibank locations nationwide, as well as at several other banks. The service charge ranges between 1.5% and 2%; checks come in denominations of $20, $50, $100, $500, and $1,000. Call ✆ **800/732-1322** for information. AAA members can obtain Visa checks for a $9.95 fee (for checks up to $1,500) at most AAA offices or by calling ✆ **866/339-3378. MasterCard** also offers traveler's checks. Call ✆ **800/223-9920** for a location near you.

CREDIT CARDS

Credit cards are another safe way to carry money. They also provide a convenient record of all your expenses, and they generally offer relatively good exchange rates. You can also withdraw cash advances from your credit cards at banks or ATMs, provided you know your PIN. If you don't know yours, call the number on the back of your credit card and ask the bank to send it to you. It usually takes 5 to 7 business days, though some banks will provide the number over the phone if you tell them your mother's maiden name or some other personal information. Credit cards still may be the smart way to go when you factor in things like exorbitant ATM fees and service fees you'll pay with traveler's checks.

3 When to Go

While summer is the sunniest season in Portland and the obvious time to visit, it's also the most crowded time of year. Although the city is not yet so popular that you can't usually get a room in town at the last minute, you'll definitely have more choices if you plan ahead. If, on the other hand, you visit in one of the rainier months, between October and May, you'll find lower hotel room rates and almost as much to see and do.

THE WEATHER

This is the section you've all been looking for. You've all heard about the horrible weather in the Northwest. It rains all year, right? Wrong! The Portland area has some of the most beautiful summer weather in the country—warm, sunny days with clear blue skies and cool nights perfect for sleeping. During July, August, and September, it almost never rains.

And the rest of the year? Well, yes, it rains in those months and it rains regularly. But the rain is generally a fine mist—not the torrential downpours most people associate with the word *rain*. The average annual rainfall in Portland is less than it is in New York; Boston; Washington, D.C.; or Atlanta (but Portland has more days of rain and more cloudy days). A raincoat and a sweater or jacket are all a way of life in this part of the country, with Gore-Tex the preferred material. Portlanders seldom use umbrellas since the rain is rarely more than a steady drizzle.

Winters here aren't too bad, either. They're warmer than in the Northeast, although there is snow in the nearby mountains. In fact, there's so much snow on Mount Hood—only 90 minutes from downtown Portland—that you can ski right through the summer.

All in all, the best months to visit are August and September, and if you're headed to the coast, September is definitely the best month. Octobers can be very pleasant if the rainy season starts slowly. Even in the spring there are often weeks, here and there, when the sun shines, and even when it doesn't, the spring flower displays around Portland are so colorful that you hardly notice that the skies are gray.

Of course, you're skeptical, so here are the statistics.

Portland's Average Temperature & Days of Rain

	Jan	Feb	Mar	Apr	May	June	July	Aug	Sept	Oct	Nov	Dec
Temp. (°F)	40	43	46	50	57	63	68	67	63	54	46	41
Temp. (°C)	4	6	8	10	14	17	20	19	17	12	8	5
Rain (Days)	18	16	17	14	12	10	4	5	8	13	18	19

PORTLAND CALENDAR OF EVENTS

For a calendar of special events in and around Portland, contact the **Portland Oregon Visitors Association** (see section 1 of this chapter), which lists special events in a couple of its publications and also on its website (**www.travel portland.com**). The *Oregonian* newspaper also lists special events at **www.oregonlive.com**. To find out what's going on during your visit, pick up a free copy of *Willamette Week* (online at **www.wweek.com**) or buy the Friday or Sunday *Oregonian.* Some of the larger and more popular special and free events are listed there.

February

The Portland International Film Festival, Portland. Although not one of the country's top film festivals, plenty of interesting foreign films and documentaries are shown. Screenings are held at various theaters around the city. ℭ **503/221-1156;** www.nwfilm.org. Last 2 weeks of February.

May

Mother's Day Rhododendron Show, Portland. At Crystal Springs Rhododendron Garden, blooming rhododendrons and azaleas transform the tranquil garden into a mass of blazing color. ℭ **503/771-8386.** Mother's Day.

Memorial Day Wine Tastings, throughout the wine country surrounding Portland. This is one of 2 weekends celebrated by Willamette Valley wineries with special tastings and events. Many wineries not usually open to the public open on this weekend. ℭ **503/646-2985;** www.willamettewines.com. Memorial Day weekend.

June

Portland Rose Festival. From its beginnings back in 1888, the Rose Festival has blossomed into Portland's biggest celebration. The festivities now span nearly a month and include the nation's second-largest all-floral parade, rose queen contest, music festival, art festival, and dragon-boat races. Contact the Portland Rose Festival Association (ℭ **503/227-2681;** www.rosefestival.org) for tickets and information. Most of the events (some of which are free) take place during the middle 2 weeks of June, and hotel rooms can be hard to come by, so plan ahead.

Portland Arts Festival (ℭ **503/227-2681;** www.rosefestival.org), South Park Blocks at Portland State University. More than 150 artists are juried into this fine arts-and-crafts show, ensuring good-quality art-buying opportunities. Music, theater, and local wines and microbrews, too. Mid-June.

July

Fourth of July Fireworks, Vancouver, Washington. Vancouver, which is part of the Portland metropolitan area, hosts the biggest fireworks display west of the Mississippi. ✆ **877/600-0800** or 360/750-1553. July 4.

Waterfront Blues Festival, Portland. This is Portland's biggest summer party and takes place in Tom McCall Waterfront Park. Expect lots of big names in blues. ✆ **503/973-FEST;** www. waterfrontbluesfest.com. Fourth of July weekend.

Summer Concert Series, Oregon Zoo (✆ **503/226-1561;** www.oregonzoo.org). Regional and nationally-known performers appear at the zoo's amphitheater. Ticket prices range from $9.50 to $26. July and August.

Noon Tunes (✆ **503/223-1613**), Pioneer Courthouse Square. This is a series of free lunchtime concerts featuring everything from classical music to bluegrass to jazz to Japanese taiko drumming. They're held every Tuesday and Thursday in July and August.

Oregon Brewers Festival, Tom McCall Waterfront Park. One of the country's largest festivals of independent craft brewers features lots of local and international microbrews and music. ✆ **503/778-5917;** www.oregonbrewfest.com. Last weekend in July.

August

Mount Hood Jazz Festival, Gresham (less than 30 min. from Portland). For the jazz fan, this is the most important festival of the summer. ✆ **503/491-5950;** www.mthoodjazz.com. Early August.

The Bite of Oregon, Tom McCall Waterfront Park (✆ **503/248-0600;** www.biteoforegon.com). Portland's finest restaurants serve up sample portions of their specialties at this food and music festival. It's a true gustatory extravaganza and also includes wine tasting. This is a benefit for the Special Olympics. Mid-August.

September

Reptile and Amphibian Show, Oregon Museum of Science and Industry (✆ **503/797-6674;** www.omsi.edu). Hundreds of reptiles and amphibians are brought in for a holiday weekend show that's the biggest of its kind in the Northwest. Kids love this venomous event! Labor Day weekend.

Oktoberfest, Oaks Park Amusement Center (✆ **503/233-5777;** www.oakspark.com). A large and crowded Oktoberfest with lots of polka in the beer hall. Late September.

October

Howloween, Oregon Zoo (© **503/226-1561**; www.oregonzoo. org). Sort of a trick-or-treat scavenger hunt, with lots of activities for kids. Last weekend in October.

Portland Marathon, downtown Portland (© **503/226-1111**; www.portlandmarathon.org). Features a variety of competitions, including a 26.2-mile walk, a 5-mile run, and a kid's 2-mile run. Early October.

November

Wine Country Thanksgiving, Willamette Valley. About 30 miles outside of Portland, more than two dozen wineries open their doors for tastings of new releases, usually with food and live music. © **503/646-2985**; www.willamettewines.com. Thanksgiving weekend.

Christmas at Pittock Mansion, Pittock Mansion (© **503/823-3624**; www.pittockmansion.org). Each year, this grand French Renaissance–style château is decorated according to an annual theme. Thanksgiving to end of December.

December

Holiday Parade of Ships, Willamette and Columbia rivers. Boats decked out in fanciful holiday lights parade and circle on the rivers after nightfall. www.christmasships.org. Mid-December.

Zoo Lights, Oregon Zoo (© **503/226-1561**; www.oregonzoo.org). One of Portland's most impressive holiday light shows is at the Oregon Zoo. No, they don't put lights on the animals, but just about everything else seems to get covered. Month of December (closed Dec 24–25).

4 Travel Insurance, Health & Safety

Check your existing insurance policies and credit card coverage before you buy travel insurance. You may already be covered for lost luggage, canceled tickets, or medical expenses.

The cost of travel insurance varies widely, depending on the cost and length of your trip, your age and health, and the type of trip you're taking, but expect to pay between 5% and 8% of the vacation itself. You can get estimates from various providers through **Insure MyTrip.com.**

TRIP-CANCELLATION INSURANCE Trip-cancellation insurance will help retrieve your money if you have to back out of a trip or depart early, or if your travel supplier goes bankrupt. Permissible reasons for trip cancellation can range from sickness to natural disasters to the State Department declaring a destination unsafe for travel. In this unstable world, trip-cancellation insurance is a good buy if you're purchasing tickets well in advance—who knows what the state of the world, or of your airline, will be in 9 months? Insurance policy details vary, so read the fine print—and make sure that your airline or cruise line is on the list of carriers covered in case of bankruptcy. A good resource is **"Travel Guard Alerts,"** a list of companies considered high-risk by Travel Guard International (see website below). Protect yourself further by paying for the insurance with a credit card—by law, consumers can get their money back on goods and services not received if they report the loss within 60 days after the charge is listed on their credit card statement.

For more information, contact one of the following recommended insurers: **Access America** (② 866/807-3982; www.access america.com), **Travel Guard International** (② 800/826-4919; www. travelguard.com), **Travel Insured International** (② 800/243-3174; www.travelinsured.com), or **Travelex Insurance Services** (② 888/ 457-4602; www.travelex-insurance.com).

MEDICAL INSURANCE   Most health insurance policies cover you if you get sick away from home—but verify that you're covered before you depart, particularly if you're insured by an HMO. If you require additional medical insurance, try **MEDEX Assistance** (② 410/453-6300; www.medexassist.com) or **Travel Assistance International** (② 800/821-2828; www.travelassistance.com; for general information on services, call the company's **Worldwide Assistance Services, Inc.,** at ② 800/777-8710).

LOST-LUGGAGE INSURANCE   On domestic flights, checked baggage is covered up to $2,500 per ticketed passenger. On international flights (including U.S. portions of international trips), baggage coverage is limited to approximately $9.07 per pound, up to approximately $635 per checked bag. If you plan to check items more valuable than what's covered by the standard liability, see if your homeowner's policy covers your valuables, get baggage insurance as part of your comprehensive travel-insurance package, or buy Travel Guard's BagTrak product. Be sure to take any valuables or irreplaceable items with you in your carry-on luggage because many valuables aren't covered by airline policies.

If your luggage is lost, immediately file a lost-luggage claim at the airport, detailing the luggage contents. Most airlines require that you report delayed, damaged, or lost baggage within 4 hours of arrival. The airlines are required to deliver luggage, once found, directly to your house or destination free of charge.

STAYING HEALTHY If you're worried about getting sick while away from home, consider purchasing **medical travel insurance** (see below) and remember to carry your ID card in your purse or wallet at all times. In most cases, your existing health plan will provide the coverage you need.

WHAT TO DO IF YOU GET SICK AWAY FROM HOME

If you get sick, consider asking your hotel concierge to recommend a local doctor—even his or her own. You can also try an urgent-care facility or a local hospital, many of which have walk-in clinics for emergency cases that are not life threatening. You may not get immediate attention, but you won't pay the high price of an emergency-room visit. Alternatively, search out an urgent-care center. These small medical facilities have doctors on staff who primarily treat walk-in patients who have problems that are not life threatening.

If you suffer from a chronic illness, consult your doctor before your departure. For conditions like epilepsy, diabetes, or heart problems, wear a **MedicAlert identification tag** (© 888/633-4298; www.medicalert.org), which will immediately alert doctors to your condition and give them access to your records through Medic-Alert's 24-hour hot line.

Pack **prescription medications** in your carry-on luggage, and carry prescription medications in their original containers, with pharmacy labels—otherwise, they won't make it through airport security. Also carry copies of your prescriptions in case you lose your pills or run out. Don't forget an extra pair of contact lenses or prescription glasses.

For domestic trips, most reliable health-care plans provide coverage if you get sick away from home. See "Medical Insurance," under "Travel Insurance, Health & Safety," above.

5 Specialized Travel Resources

TRAVELERS WITH DISABILITIES

Always mention your disability when making airline reservations. Airline policies differ regarding wheelchairs and Seeing Eye dogs.

Most hotels now offer wheelchair-accessible accommodations, and some of the larger and more expensive properties also offer TDD telephones and other amenities for the hearing and sight impaired.

The public transit systems found in most Oregon cities either have regular vehicles that are accessible for riders with disabilities or offer special transportation services for people with disabilities.

For anyone who is hearing impaired, **Oregon State Parks** has a TT information line (© **800/858-9659**) that provides recreation and camping information.

If you plan to visit any of Crater Lake National Park or Lewis & Clark National and State Historical Parks, you can avail yourself of the **Golden Access Passport,** which gives free lifetime entrance to all national parks, monuments, wildlife refuges, historic sites, and recreation areas for persons who are visually impaired or permanently disabled, regardless of age. You may pick up a Golden Access Passport at any NPS visitor center by showing proof of medically determined disability and eligibility for receiving benefits under federal law. For more information, go to www.nps.gov/fees_passes.htm or call © **888/467-2757.**

Many travel agencies offer customized tours and itineraries for travelers with disabilities. **Flying Wheels Travel** (© **507/451-5005;** www.flyingwheelstravel.com) offers escorted tours and cruises that emphasize sports and private tours in minivans with lifts. **Access-Able Travel Source** (© **303/232-2979;** www.access-able.com) offers extensive access information and advice for traveling around the world with disabilities. **Accessible Journeys** (© **800/846-4537** or 610/521-0339; www.disabilitytravel.com) caters specifically to slow walkers and wheelchair travelers and their families and friends.

Avis Rent a Car has an "Avis Access" program that offers such services as a dedicated 24-hour toll-free number (© **888/879-4273**) for customers with special travel needs; special car features such as swivel seats, spinner knobs, and hand controls; and accessible bus service.

Organizations that offer assistance to disabled travelers include **MossRehab** (www.mossresourcenet.org), which provides a library of accessible-travel resources online; the **American Foundation for the Blind (AFB)** (© **800/232-5463;** www.afb.org), a referral resource for the blind or visually impaired that includes information on traveling with Seeing Eye dogs; and **SATH (Society for Accessible Travel & Hospitality)** (© **212/447-7284;** www.sath.org; annual membership fees: $45 adults, $30 seniors and students), which offers a wealth of travel resources for all types of disabilities and informed recommendations on destinations, access guides, travel agents, tour operators, vehicle rentals, and companion services.

For more information specifically targeted to travelers with disabilities, the community website **iCan** (www.icanonline.net/channels/travel) has destination guides and several regular columns on accessible travel.

GAYS & LESBIANS

Gay and lesbian travelers visiting Portland should be sure to pick up a free copy of *Just Out* (© **503/236-1252;** www.justout.com), a bimonthly newspaper for the gay community. You can usually find copies at **Powell's Books,** 1005 W. Burnside St. Another publication to look for is *Portland's Gay & Lesbian Community Yellow Pages* (© **503/230-7701;** www.pdxgayyellowpages.com), which is also usually available at Powell's.

The **International Gay and Lesbian Travel Association (IGLTA)** (© **800/448-8550** or 954/776-2626; www.iglta.org) is the trade association for the gay and lesbian travel industry, and offers an online directory of gay- and lesbian-friendly travel businesses; go to their website and click on "Members."

FOR SENIORS

Mention the fact that you're a senior when you make your travel reservations. Although all the major U.S. airlines except America West have canceled their senior discount and coupon book programs, many hotels still offer lower rates for seniors. In most cities, people over the age of 60 qualify for reduced admission to theaters, museums, and other attractions, and discounted fares on public transportation.

Members of **AARP** (formerly known as the American Association of Retired Persons), 601 E St. NW, Washington, DC 20049 (© **888/687-2277;** www.aarp.org), get discounts on hotels, airfares, and car rentals. AARP offers members a wide range of benefits, including *AARP: The Magazine* and a monthly newsletter. Anyone over 50 can join.

The U.S. National Park Service offers a **Golden Age Passport** that gives seniors 62 and older lifetime entrance to most national parks and monuments for a one-time processing fee of $10. It must be purchased in person at any NPS facility that charges an entrance fee. Besides free entry, a Golden Age Passport offers a 50% discount on federal-use fees charged for such facilities as camping, swimming, parking, boat launching, and tours. For more information, go to www.nps.gov/fees_passes.htm or call © **888/467-2757.**

Many reliable agencies and organizations target the 50-plus market. **Elderhostel** (© **877/426-8056;** www.elderhostel.org) arranges study programs for those aged 55 and over (and a spouse or companion of any age). **ElderTreks** (© **800/741-7956;** www.elder treks.com), restricted to travelers 50 and older, offers small-group tours to off-the-beaten-path or adventure-travel locations.

FAMILY TRAVEL

If you have enough trouble simply getting your kids out of the house in the morning, dragging them thousands of miles away may seem like an insurmountable challenge. But family travel can be immensely rewarding, giving you new ways of seeing the world through smaller pairs of eyes.

To locate those accommodations, restaurants, and attractions that are particularly kid-friendly, refer to the "Kids" icon throughout this guide.

Families traveling in Oregon should be sure to take note of family admission fees at many museums and other attractions. These admission prices are often less than what it would cost for individual tickets for the whole family. At hotels and motels, children usually stay free if they share their parents' room and no extra bed is required, and sometimes they also get to eat for free in the hotel dining room. Be sure to ask.

Recommended family travel Internet sites include **Family Travel Forum** (www.familytravelforum.com), a comprehensive site that offers customized trip planning, and **Family Travel Network** (www. familytravelnetwork.com), an award-winning site that offers travel features, deals, and tips.

6 Planning Your Trip Online

SURFING FOR AIRFARES

The "big three" online travel agencies, **Expedia.com, Travelocity. com,** and **Orbitz.com,** sell most of the air tickets bought on the Internet. (Canadian travelers should try expedia.ca and Travelocity.ca; U.K. residents can go for expedia.co.uk and opodo.co.uk.). **Kayak.com** is also gaining popularity and uses a sophisticated search engine (developed at MIT). Each has different business deals with the airlines and may offer different fares on the same flights, so it's wise to shop around.

Also remember to check **airline websites,** especially those for low-fare carriers such as Southwest and JetBlue, whose fares are often misreported or simply missing from travel agency websites. Even with major airlines, you can often shave a few bucks from a fare by booking directly through the airline. But you'll get these discounts only by

booking online: Most airlines now offer online-only fares that even their phone agents know nothing about. For the websites of airlines that fly to and from Oregon, go to "Getting There," p. 24.

Great **last-minute deals** are available through free weekly e-mail services provided directly by the airlines. Most of these are announced on Tuesday or Wednesday and must be purchased online. Most are valid only for travel that weekend, but some (such as Southwest's) can be booked weeks or months in advance. Sign up for weekly e-mail alerts at airline websites or check mega-sites that compile comprehensive lists of last-minute specials, such as **Smarter Travel** (smartertravel.com). For last-minute trips, **site59.com** and **lastminutetravel. com** in the U.S. and **lastminute.com** in Europe often have better air-and-hotel package deals than the major-label sites.

If you're willing to give up some control over your flight details, use what is called an **"opaque" fare service** like **Priceline** (www. priceline.com; www.priceline.co.uk for Europeans) or its smaller competitor **Hotwire** (www.hotwire.com). Both offer rock-bottom prices in exchange for travel on a "mystery airline" at a mysterious time of day, often with a mysterious change of planes en route. The mystery airlines are all major, well-known carriers. Your chances of getting a 6am or 11pm flight, however, are still pretty high. Hotwire tells you flight prices before you buy; Priceline usually has better deals than Hotwire, but you have to play their "name our price" game or pick exact flights, times, and airlines from a list of offers. If you're new at this, **BiddingForTravel** (www.biddingfortravel.com) does a good job of demystifying Priceline's prices and strategies.

SURFING FOR HOTELS

Shopping online for hotels is generally done one of two ways: by booking through the hotel's own website or through an independent booking agency (or a fare-service agency like Priceline; see below).

Of the "big three" sites, **Expedia** offers a long list of special deals and "virtual tours" or photos of available rooms so you can see what you're paying for. **Travelocity** posts unvarnished customer reviews and ranks its properties according to the AAA rating system. **Trip Advisor** (www.tripadvisor.com) is another excellent source of unbiased user reviews of hotels. While even the finest hotels can inspire a misleadingly poor review from a picky or crabby traveler, the body of user opinions is usually a reliable indicator.

Other reliable online booking agencies include **Hotels.com** and **Quikbook.com.** An excellent free program, **TravelAxe** (www.travel axe.net), can help you search multiple hotel sites at once, even ones you may never have heard of—and conveniently lists the total price of the room, including the taxes and service charges. Another booking site, **Travelweb** (www.travelweb.com), is partly owned by the hotels it represents (including the Hilton, Hyatt, and Starwood chains) and is therefore plugged directly into the hotels' reservations systems. Be sure to **get a confirmation number** and **make a printout** of any online booking transaction.

In the opaque website category, **Priceline** and **Hotwire** are even better for hotels than for airfares; through both, you're allowed to pick the neighborhood and quality level of your hotel before paying. Priceline's hotel product is much better at getting five-star lodging for three-star prices than at finding anything at the bottom of the scale. On the down side, many hotels stick Priceline guests in their least desirable rooms. Be sure to go to the BiddingForTravel website (see above) before bidding on a hotel room on Priceline; it features a fairly up-to-date list of hotels that Priceline uses in major cities.

SURFING FOR RENTAL CARS

For booking rental cars online, the best deals are usually found at rental-car company websites, although all the major online travel agencies also offer rental-car reservations services. Priceline and Hotwire work well for rental cars, too; the only "mystery" is which major rental company you get, and for most travelers the difference between Hertz, Avis, and Budget is negligible.

7 The 21st-Century Traveler

INTERNET ACCESS AWAY FROM HOME

Travelers have any number of ways to check their e-mail and access the Internet on the road. Of course, using your own laptop—or even a PDA (personal digital assistant) or electronic organizer with a modem—gives you the most flexibility. But even if you don't have a computer, you can still access your e-mail and even your office computer from cybercafes.

WITHOUT YOUR OWN COMPUTER

It's hard nowadays to find a city that *doesn't* have a few cybercafes. Although there's no definitive directory for cybercafes—these are independent businesses, after all—two places to start looking are at **www.cybercaptive.com** and **www.cybercafe.com**.

Aside from formal cybercafes, most **public libraries** offer access free or for a small charge.

To retrieve your e-mail, ask your **Internet service provider (ISP)** if it has a Web-based interface tied to your existing e-mail account. If your ISP doesn't have such an interface, you can use the free **mail2web** service (www.mail2web.com) to view and reply to your home e-mail. For more flexibility, you may want to open a free, Web-based e-mail account with **Yahoo! Mail** (http://mail.yahoo.com). (Microsoft's Hotmail is another popular option, but Hotmail has severe spam problems.) Your home ISP may be able to forward your e-mail to the Web-based account automatically.

WITH YOUR OWN COMPUTER

More and more hotels, cafes, and retailers are signing on as Wi-Fi (wireless fidelity) "hotspots," from where you can get high-speed connection without cable wires, networking hardware, or a phone line (see below). You can get Wi-Fi connection one of several ways. Many laptops sold in the last few years have built-in Wi-Fi capability. Mac owners have their own networking technology, Apple AirPort. For those with older computers, you can plug in an 802.11b/ **Wi-Fi card** (around $50). You sign up for wireless access service much as you do for cellphone service, through a plan offered by one of several commercial companies that have made wireless service available in airports, hotel lobbies, and coffee shops, primarily in the U.S. (followed by the U.K. and Japan). **T-Mobile Hotspot** (www. t-mobile.com/hotspot) serves up wireless connections at more than 1,000 Starbucks coffee shops nationwide. **Boingo** (www.boingo. com) and **Wayport** (www.wayport.com) have set up networks in airports and high-class hotel lobbies. To locate other hotspots that provide **free wireless networks,** go to **www.personaltelco.net/ index.cgi/WirelessCommunities**.

For dial-up access, most business-class hotels offer dataports for laptop modems, and many hotels offer free high-speed Internet access using an Ethernet network cable. **Call your hotel in advance** to see what your options are.

In addition, major Internet service providers (ISPs) have **local access numbers,** allowing you to go online by placing a local call. Check your ISP's website for information.

Wherever you go, bring a **connection kit** of the right power and phone adapters, a spare phone cord, and a spare Ethernet network cable—or find out whether your hotel supplies them to guests.

USING A CELLPHONE ACROSS THE U.S.

Just because your cellphone works at home doesn't mean it'll work elsewhere in the country (thanks to our nation's fragmented cellphone

Online Traveler's Toolbox

Veteran travelers usually carry some essential items to make their trips easier. Following is a selection of handy online tools to bookmark and use:

- **Mapquest** (www.mapquest.com). This best of the mapping sites lets you choose a specific address or destination, and, in seconds, returns a map and detailed directions.
- **Visa ATM Locator** (www.visa.com), for locations of PLUS ATMs worldwide, or **MasterCard ATM Locator** (www.mastercard.com), for locations of Cirrus ATMs worldwide.
- **Intellicast** (www.intellicast.com) and **Weather.com** (www.weather.com). Give weather forecasts for all 50 states and for cities around the world.

system). It's a good bet that your phone will work in major cities. But take a look at your wireless company's coverage map on its website before heading out—T-Mobile, Sprint, and Nextel are particularly weak in rural areas. If you need to stay in touch at a destination where you know your phone won't work, **rent** a phone that does from **InTouch USA** (✆ **800/872-7626;** www.intouchglobal.com) or a rental car location, but beware that you'll pay $1 a minute or more for airtime.

8 Getting There

BY PLANE

The major carriers to **Portland Airport** (www.flypdx.com) include **Air Canada Jazz** (✆ 888/247-2262; www.flyjazz.ca), **Alaska Airlines** (✆ 800/252-7522; www.alaskaair.com), **America West** (✆ 800/235-9292; www.americawest.com), **American** (✆ 800/433-7300; www.aa.com), **Continental** (✆ 800/523-3273; www.continental.com), **Delta** (✆ 800/221-1212; www.delta.com), **Frontier** (✆ 800/432-1359; www.frontierairlines.com), **Horizon Air** (✆ 800/547-9308; www.horizonair.com), **JetBlue Airways** (✆ 800/JETBLUE; www.jetblue.com), **Lufthansa** (✆ 800/645-3880; www.lufthansa.com), **Northwest/KLM** (✆ 800/225-2525; www.nwa.com), **Southwest** (✆ 800/435-9792; www.southwest.com), and **United** (✆ 800/864-8331; www.united.com).

GETTING THROUGH THE AIRPORT

With the federalization of airport security, screening procedures at U.S. airports are more stable and consistent than ever. Generally, you'll be fine if you arrive at the airport **1 hour** before a domestic flight and **2 hours** before an international flight.

Bring a **current, government-issued photo ID** such as a driver's license or passport. Keep your ID at the ready to present at check-in, the security checkpoint, and sometimes even the gate. (Children under 18 do not need government-issued photo IDs for domestic flights, but they do for international flights to most countries.)

Passengers with e-tickets, which have made paper tickets nearly obsolete, can beat the ticket-counter lines by using airport **electronic kiosks** or even **online check-in** from their home computers. Online check-in involves logging on to your airlines' website, accessing your reservation, and printing out your boarding pass.

If you have trouble standing for long periods of time, tell an airline employee; the airline will provide a wheelchair. Speed up security by **not wearing metal objects** such as big belt buckles. If you've got metallic body parts, a note from your doctor can prevent a long chat with the security screeners.

Federalization has stabilized **what you can carry on** and **what you can't.** The general rule is that sharp things are out. Bring food in your carry-on rather than checking it, as explosive-detection machines used on checked luggage have been known to mistake food (especially chocolate, for some reason) for bombs. Travelers in the U.S. are allowed one carry-on bag, plus a "personal item" such as a purse, briefcase, or laptop bag. The Transportation Security Administration (TSA) has issued a list of restricted items; check its website (www.tsa.gov/public/index.jsp) for details.

Airport screeners may decide that your checked luggage warrants a hand search. You can now purchase luggage locks that allow screeners to open and relock a checked bag if hand searching is necessary. Look for Travel Sentry certified locks at luggage or travel shops and Brookstone stores (you can buy them online at www.brookstone.com). Luggage inspectors can open these TSA-approved locks with a special code or key—rather than having to cut them off the suitcase, as they normally do to conduct a hand search. For more information on the locks, visit www.travelsentry.org.

FLYING FOR LESS: TIPS FOR GETTING THE BEST AIRFARES

Passengers sharing the same airplane cabin rarely pay the same fare. Travelers who need to purchase tickets at the last minute, change their itinerary at a moment's notice, or fly one-way often get stuck paying the premium rate. Here are some ways to keep your airfare costs down.

If you're flying to Portland from another city in the western U.S., check with Frontier Airlines, Alaska Airlines, Horizon Airlines, or Southwest. These airlines often have the best fares between western cities.

- Passengers who can book their ticket either **long in advance or at the last minute,** or who **fly midweek** or **at less-trafficked hours** may pay a fraction of the full fare. If your schedule is flexible, say so, and ask if you can secure a cheaper fare by changing your flight plans.

- Keep an eye on local newspapers for **promotional specials** or **fare wars,** when airlines lower prices on their most popular routes. You rarely see fare wars offered for peak travel times, but if you can travel in the off-months, you may snag a bargain.

- **Consolidators,** also known as bucket shops, are great sources for international tickets, although they usually can't beat Internet fares within North America. Start by looking in Sunday newspaper travel sections; U.S. travelers should focus on the *New York Times, Los Angeles Times,* and *Miami Herald.* Several reliable consolidators are worldwide and available online. **STA Travel** has been the world's lead consolidator for students since purchasing Council Travel, but their fares are competitive for travelers of all ages. **Air Tickets Direct** (*©* **800/778-3447;** www.airticketsdirect.com) is based in Montreal and leverages the currently weak Canadian dollar for low fares.

- Join **frequent-flier clubs.** Frequent-flier membership doesn't cost a cent, but it does entitle you to better seats, faster response to phone inquiries, and prompter service if your luggage is stolen or your flight is canceled or delayed, or if you want to change your seat.

BY CAR

The distance to Portland from Seattle is 175 miles; from Spokane, 350 miles; from Vancouver, British Columbia, 285 miles; from San Francisco, 640 miles; and from Los Angeles, 1,015 miles.

If you're driving from California, I-5 runs up through the length of the state and continues up toward the Canadian border; it will take you through both Portland and Seattle. If you're coming from the east, I-84 runs from Idaho and points east into Oregon, eventually ending in Portland.

One of the most important benefits of belonging to the **American Automobile Association** (© **800/222-4357;** www.aaa.com) is that it supplies members with emergency road service. In Portland, AAA is located at 600 SW Market St. (© **503/222-6734;** www.aaaorid.com).

BY TRAIN

Amtrak's (© **800/872-7245;** www.amtrak.com) *Coast Starlight* train connects Portland with Seattle, San Francisco, Los Angeles, and San Diego, and stops at historic **Union Station,** 800 NW Sixth Ave. (© **503/273-4860**), about 10 blocks from the heart of downtown Portland. Between Portland and Seattle there are both regular trains and modern European-style Talgo trains, which make the trip in 3½ to 4 hours vs. 4½ hours for the regular train. One-way fares on either type of train run $25 to $30. The Talgo train, called *Cascades,* runs between Eugene, Oregon, and Vancouver, British Columbia.

BY BUS

Portland is served by **Greyhound Bus Lines.** The bus station is at 550 NW Sixth Ave. (© **800/231-2222** or 503/243-2310; www.greyhound.com). From Seattle to Portland, it's around $25 one-way and $50 round-trip. The trip takes 3½ to 4½ hours.

3

Getting to Know Portland

1 Orientation

ARRIVING

BY PLANE

Portland International Airport (PDX) (© 877/739-4636 or 503/
460-4234; www.portlandairportpdx.com) is located 10 miles northeast of downtown Portland, adjacent to the Columbia River. There's
an information booth by the baggage-claim area where you can pick
up maps and brochures and find out about transportation into the
city. Many hotels near the airport provide courtesy shuttle service to
and from the airport; be sure to ask when you make a reservation.

GETTING INTO THE CITY BY CAR   If you've rented a car at
the airport and want to reach central Portland, follow signs for
downtown. These signs will take you first to I-205 and then I-84
West, which brings you to the Willamette River. Take the Morrison
Bridge exit to cross the river. The trip takes about 20 minutes and is
entirely on interstates. For more information on renting a car, see
section 2 of this chapter, "Getting Around," below.

**GETTING INTO THE CITY BY TAXI, SHUTTLE, BUS, OR
LIGHT RAIL**   If you haven't rented a car at the airport, the best
way to get into town is to take the **Airport MAX (Red Line)** light-
rail system. This light-rail line operates daily roughly every 15 minutes between 5am and midnight, and the trip from the airport to
Pioneer Courthouse Square in downtown Portland takes approximately 35 minutes. (All but one or two of the downtown hotels lie
within 4 or 5 blocks of the square; plan on walking since taxis in
Portland don't generally cruise for fares. Folks arriving with a lot of
luggage will be better off taking a cab or shuttle van from the airport.) The fare is $1.80. For information on this service, contact
TriMet (© 503/238-7433; www.trimet.org).

A taxi to downtown generally costs between $30 and $35.

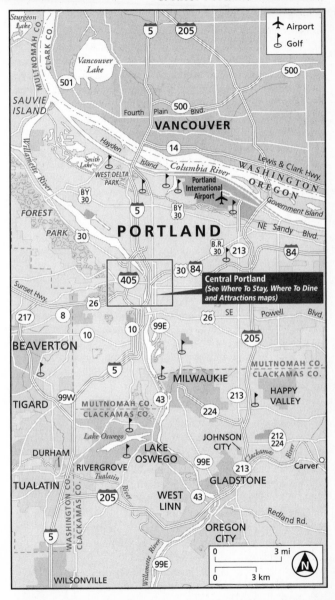

Central Portland
(See Where To Stay, Where To Dine and Attractions maps)

BY TRAIN/BUS

Amtrak trains stop at the historic **Union Station,** 800 NW Sixth Ave. (© **800/872-7245** or 503/273-4860; www.amtrak.com), about 10 blocks from the heart of downtown Portland. Taxis are usually waiting to meet trains and can take you to your hotel. Alternatively, you might be able to get your hotel to send a van to pick you up, or, if you are renting a car from a downtown car-rental office, the agency will usually pick you up at the station. Public buses stop in the block south of the station (toward downtown) and are free within the downtown area.

The **Greyhound Bus Lines** station is at 550 NW Sixth Ave. (© **800/231-2222** or 503/243-2310; www.greyhound.com) on the north side of downtown near Union Station. As with getting into downtown from the train station, there is no charge to ride any public city bus if you catch it outside the Greyhound terminal, which is within Portland's Fareless Square area.

Although you could easily walk from the station into the heart of downtown, you have to pass through a somewhat rough neighborhood for a few blocks. This area is currently undergoing a renaissance and is not nearly as bad as it once was.

VISITOR INFORMATION

The **Portland Oregon Visitors Association (POVA) Information Center,** 701 SW Sixth Ave. (© **877/678-5263** or 503/275-8355; www.travelportland.com), is in Pioneer Courthouse Square in downtown Portland. There's also an information booth by the baggage-claim area at the Portland Airport.

CITY LAYOUT

Portland is in northwestern Oregon at the confluence of the Columbia and Willamette rivers. To the west are the West Hills, which rise to more than 1,000 feet. Some 90 miles west of the West Hills are the spectacular Oregon coast and the Pacific Ocean. To the east are rolling hills that extend to the Cascade Range, about 50 miles away. The most prominent peak in this section of the Cascades is Mount Hood (11,235 ft.), a dormant volcanic peak that looms over the city on clear days. From many parts of Portland it's also possible to see Mount St. Helens, a volcano that erupted violently in 1980.

With about two million people in the entire metropolitan area, Portland remains a relatively small city. This is especially evident when you begin to explore the compact downtown area. Nearly everything is accessible on foot, and the city authorities do everything they can to encourage walking.

MAIN ARTERIES & STREETS I-84 (Banfield Fwy. or Expwy.) enters Portland from the east. East of the city is **I-205,** which bypasses downtown Portland and runs past the airport. **I-5** runs through on a north-south axis, passing along the east bank of the Willamette River directly across from downtown. **I-405** circles around the west and south sides of downtown. **U.S. 26 (Sunset Hwy.)** leaves downtown heading west toward Beaverton and the coast. **Oregon Hwy. 217** runs south from U.S. 26 in Beaverton.

The most important artery within Portland is **Burnside Street.** This is the dividing line between north and south Portland. Dividing the city from east to west is the **Willamette River,** which is crossed by eight bridges in the downtown area. From north to south these bridges are the Fremont, Broadway, Steel, Burnside, Morrison, Hawthorne, Marquam, and Ross Island. Additional bridges beyond the downtown area include the Sellwood Bridge, located between downtown and Lake Oswego, and the St. John's Bridge, which connects northwest Portland with north Portland.

For the sake of convenience, we have defined downtown Portland as the 300-block area within the **Fareless Square.** This is the area (shaded in on the map on p. 42) in which you can ride for free on the city's public buses, the MAX light-rail system, and the Portland Streetcar. In downtown, the Fareless Square is bounded by I-405 on the west and south, by Irving Street on the north, and by the Willamette River on the east. A Fareless Square extension also allows transit riders to travel free between downtown Portland and both the Oregon Convention Center and Lloyd Center Mall. There is no charge to ride either the MAX light-rail trolleys or any of the buses that connect downtown with the Rose Quarter and Lloyd District across the Willamette River in northeast Portland.

FINDING AN ADDRESS Finding an address in Portland can be easy. Almost all addresses in Portland, and for miles beyond, include a map quadrant—NE (northeast), SW (southwest), and so forth. The dividing line between east and west is the Willamette River; between north and south it's Burnside Street. Any downtown address will be labeled either SW (southwest) or NW (northwest). An exception to this rule is the area known as North Portland, which is the area across the Willamette River from downtown going toward Jantzen Beach. Streets here have a plain "North" designation. Also, Burnside Street is designated either "East" or "West."

Avenues run north-south and streets run east-west. Street names are the same on both sides of the Willamette River. Consequently,

Fun Fact **Did You Know?**

- The flasher in the famous "Expose Yourself to Art" poster is none other than Bud Clark, the former mayor of Portland.
- Portland is the only city in the United States with an extinct volcano within the city limits (Mount Tabor).
- Matt Groening, creator of *The Simpsons,* got his start in Portland.
- More Asian elephants have been born in Portland (at the Oregon Zoo) than in any other city in North America.
- Twenty downtown water fountains were a gift to the city from teetotaling early-20th-century timber baron Simon Benson, who wanted his mill workers to have something other than alcohol to drink during the day.

there is a Southwest Yamhill Street and a Southeast Yamhill Street. In northwest Portland, street names are alphabetical going north from Burnside to Wilson. Naito Parkway is the street nearest the Willamette River on the west side, and Water Avenue is the nearest on the east side. Beyond these are numbered avenues. On the west side you'll also find Broadway and Park Avenue between Sixth Avenue and Ninth Avenue. With each block, the addresses increase by 100, beginning at the Willamette River for avenues and at Burnside Street for streets. Odd numbers are generally on the west and north sides of the street, and even numbers on the east and south sides.

Here's an example: You want to go to 1327 SW Ninth Ave. Because it's in the 1300 block, you'll find it 13 blocks south of Burnside and, because it's an odd number, on the west side of the street.

STREET MAPS   Stop by the **Portland Oregon Visitors Association Information Center,** 701 SW Sixth Ave., Suite 1 (© **877/678-5263** or 503/275-9750; www.travelportland.com), in Pioneer Courthouse Square in downtown Portland for a free map of the city.

Powell's City of Books, 1005 W. Burnside St. (© **866/201-7601** or 503/228-4651), has an excellent free map of downtown that includes a walking-tour route and information on many of the sights you'll pass along the way.

Members of the **American Automobile Association (AAA)** can get a free map of the city at the AAA offices at 600 SW Market St. (*©* **503/222-6734;** www.aaaorid.com).

PORTLAND NEIGHBORHOODS IN BRIEF

Portland's neighborhoods are mostly dictated by geography. The Willamette River forms a natural dividing line between the eastern and western portions of the city, while the Columbia River forms a boundary with the state of Washington on the north. The West Hills, comprising Portland's prime residential neighborhoods, are a beautiful backdrop for this attractive city. Covered in evergreens, the hills rise to a height of 1,000 feet at the edge of downtown. Within these hills are the Oregon Zoo, the International Rose Test Garden, the Japanese Garden, and several other attractions.

For a map of Portland neighborhoods, turn to the "Portland Attractions" map on p. 78.

Downtown   This term usually refers to the business and shopping district south of Burnside and north of Jackson Street between the Willamette River and 13th Avenue. Here you'll find a dozen or more high-end hotels, dozens of restaurants of all types, and loads of shopping (including the major department stores). Within downtown's **Cultural District** (along Broadway and the South Park blocks) are most of the city's performing arts venues and a couple of museums.

Skidmore Historic District   Also known as Old Town, this is Portland's original commercial core and centers on Southwest Ankeny Street and Southwest First Avenue. Many of the restored buildings have become retail stores, but despite the presence of the **Saturday Market,** the neighborhood has never become a popular shopping district, mostly because of its welfare hotels, missions, street people, and drug dealing. However, with its many clubs and bars, it is the city's main nightlife district. The neighborhood is safe during the day, but visitors should exercise caution at night.

Chinatown   Portland has had a Chinatown almost since its earliest days. This small area, with its numerous Chinese groceries and restaurants, is wedged between the Pearl District and the Skidmore Historic District, and is entered through the colorful Chinatown Gate at West Burnside Street and Fourth Avenue. The neighborhood's main attraction is the impressive **Portland Classical Chinese Garden.** Because of its proximity to bars on West Burnside Street and the homeless missions and welfare hotels in Old Town, this is not a good neighborhood to explore late at night.

The Pearl District This neighborhood of galleries, residential and business lofts, cafes, breweries, and shops is bounded by the North Park blocks, Northrup Street, I-405, and Burnside Street. Crowds of people come here on **First Thursday** (the first Thurs of every month), when the galleries and other businesses are open late. This is Portland's hip urban loft scene and one of the city's main upscale-restaurant neighborhoods.

Northwest/Nob Hill Located along Northwest 23rd and Northwest 21st avenues, this is one of Portland's two most fashionable neighborhoods. Here you'll find many of the city's best restaurants (mostly along NW 21st Ave.), as well as lots of cafes, boutiques, and national chain stores. Surrounding the two main business streets of the neighborhood are blocks of restored Victorian homes on shady tree-lined streets. This is where you'll find the city's liveliest street scene.

Irvington Though neither as attractive nor as large as the Northwest/Nob Hill neighborhood, Irvington, centered on Broadway in northeast Portland, is almost as hip. For several blocks along Broadway (around NE 15th Ave.) you'll find interesting boutiques and numerous good, inexpensive restaurants.

Hawthorne/Belmont District This enclave of southeast Portland is full of eclectic boutiques, moderately priced restaurants, and hip college students from nearby **Reed College.** Just south of Hawthorne Boulevard, beginning at Southeast 12th Avenue, you'll find the interesting **Ladd's Addition** neighborhood, which has five rose gardens and a great pastry shop. Belmont Street, just north of Hawthorne Boulevard, and Division Street, to the south, are two of the city's up-and-coming hip neighborhoods.

Sellwood/Westmoreland Situated in southeast Portland, this is the city's antiques district and contains many restored Victorian houses. Just north of the Sellwood antiques district, surrounding the intersection of Southeast Milwaukie Avenue and Southeast Bybee Boulevard, you'll find the heart of the Eastmoreland neighborhood, home to numerous good restaurants.

2 Getting Around

BY PUBLIC TRANSPORTATION

FREE RIDES Portland is committed to keeping its downtown uncongested and to this end has invested heavily in its public transportation system. The single greatest innovation and best reason to ride the TriMet public buses, the MAX light-rail system, and the

Portland Streetcar is that they're free within an area known as the **Fareless Square.** That's right, free!

There are 300 blocks of downtown included in the Fareless Square, and as long as you stay within the boundaries, you don't pay a cent. The Fareless Square covers the area between I-405 on the south and west, Hoyt Street on the north, and the Willamette River on the east. The Fareless Square extension also makes it possible to take public transit (either the bus or the MAX light-rail trolley) between downtown Portland and both the Rose Quarter (site of the Oregon Convention Center) and the Lloyd District (site of the Lloyd Center Mall), which are both across the Willamette River in northeast Portland.

BY BUS   TriMet buses operate daily over an extensive network. You can pick up the *TriMet Guide,* which lists all the bus routes with times, or individual route maps and time schedules, at the **TriMet Customer Assistance Office,** behind and beneath the waterfall fountain at Pioneer Courthouse Square (*©* **503/238-7433;** www.trimet.org). The office is open Monday through Friday from 8:30am to 5:30pm. Bus and MAX passes and transit information are also available at area Fred Meyer, Safeway, and most Albertson grocery stores. Nearly all TriMet buses pass through the Transit Mall on Southwest Fifth Avenue and Southwest Sixth Avenue.

Outside the Fareless Square, adult fares on TriMet buses, MAX light-rail trains, and Portland Streetcars are $1.50 or $1.80, depending on how far you travel. Seniors 65 years and older pay 70¢ with valid proof of age; children 7 through 18 pay $1.20. You can also make free transfers between the bus and both the MAX light-rail system and the Portland Streetcar. All-day tickets costing $3.75 are good for travel to all zones and are valid on buses, MAX, and streetcars. These tickets can be purchased from any bus driver or at MAX stops.

BY LIGHT RAIL   The Metropolitan Area Express (MAX) is Portland's aboveground light-rail system that connects downtown Portland with the airport, the eastern suburb of Gresham, the western suburbs of Beaverton and Hillsboro, and North Portland. MAX is basically a modern trolley, but there are also replicas of vintage trolley cars (*©* **503/323-7363**). Between March and December, the vintage trolleys operate between downtown Portland and the Lloyd Center on Sundays; year-round, they operate along the Portland Streetcar line on Saturdays and Sundays. One of the most convenient places to catch the MAX is at Pioneer Courthouse Square. The MAX light-rail system crosses the Transit Mall on Southwest Morrison Street and Southwest Yamhill Street. Transfers to the bus are free.

As with the bus, MAX is free within the Fareless Square, which includes all the downtown area. A Fareless Square extension also makes it possible to ride the MAX between downtown Portland and both the Rose Quarter (site of the Oregon Convention Center) and the Lloyd District (site of the Lloyd Center Mall). Both are across the Willamette River in northeast Portland. If you are traveling outside of the Fareless Square, be sure to buy your ticket and stamp it in the time-punch machine on the platform before you board MAX. There are ticket-vending machines at all MAX stops that tell you how much to pay for your destination; these machines also give change. The MAX driver cannot sell tickets. Fares are the same as on buses. There are ticket inspectors who randomly check to make sure passengers have stamped tickets.

The **Portland Streetcar** (© **503/238-RIDE;** www.portlandstreet car.org) operates between RiverPlace on the waterfront at the south end of downtown through the Pearl District to the Nob Hill neighborhood. The route takes in not only the attractions of the Cultural District, but also all the restaurants and great shopping in the Pearl District and along Northwest 21st and 23rd avenues, which makes this streetcar a great way for visitors to get from downtown (where most of the hotels are located) to the neighborhoods with the greatest concentrations of restaurants. On Saturdays and Sundays, vintage streetcars operate free of charge (donations are encouraged). Streetcar fares for trips outside the Fareless Square are $1.50 for adults, $1.20 for youths, and 70¢ for seniors.

BY CAR
CAR RENTALS   Portland is a compact city, and public transit will get you to most attractions within its limits. However, if you are planning to explore outside the city—and Portland's greatest attractions, such as Mount Hood and the Columbia River Gorge, lie not in the city itself, but in the countryside within an hour of the city— you'll definitely need a car.

The major car-rental companies are all represented in Portland and have desks at Portland International Airport, which is the most convenient place to pick up a car. There are also many independent and smaller car-rental agencies listed in the Portland Yellow Pages. Currently, weekly rates for an economy car in July (high-season rates) are around $150 with no discounts. Expect lower rates in the rainy months.

On the ground floor of the airport parking deck, across the street from the baggage-claim area, you'll find the following companies:

Avis (📞 **800/831-2847** or 503/249-4950; www.avis.com), **Budget** (📞 **800/527-0700** or 503/249-4556; www.budget.com), **Dollar** (📞 **800/800-3365** or 503/249-4793; www.dollar.com), **Enterprise** (📞 **800/261-7331** or 503/692-8400; www.enterprise.com), and **Hertz** (📞 **800/654-3131** or 503/249-8216; www.hertz.com). Outside the airport, but with desks adjacent to the other car-rental desks, are **Alamo** (📞 **800/327-9633** or 503/249-4900; www.go alamo.com), **National** (📞 **800/227-7368** or 503/249-4900; www. nationalcar.com), and **Thrifty** (📞 **800/847-4389** or 503/254-6563; www.thrifty.com).

PARKING   Throughout most of downtown Portland and the Pearl District, you won't find any parking meters on the streets. However, in the middle of every block you will find an electronic parking meter that takes coins, credit cards, and debit cards. These machines issue little parking receipts that you then have to tape in the curbside window of your car. Although a bit inconvenient, this system allows you to buy time while parked in one space and still use your remaining time if you move your car to another space. In most parts of town, you don't have to feed the meters after 7pm or on Sunday.

The best parking deal in town is at the **Smart Park** garages, where the cost is 95¢ per hour for the first 4 hours (but after that the hourly rate jumps to $3, so you'd be well advised to move your car), $2 for the entire evening after 6pm, or $5 to $6 all day on the weekends. Look for the red, white, and black signs featuring Les Park, the friendly parking attendant. You'll find Smart Park garages at First Avenue and Jefferson Street, Fourth Avenue and Yamhill Street, 10th Avenue and Yamhill Street, Third Avenue and Alder Street, O'Bryant Square, and Naito Parkway and Davis Street. More than 200 downtown merchants also validate Smart Park tickets for 2 hours if you spend at least $25, so don't forget to take your ticket along with you.

SPECIAL DRIVING RULES   You may turn right on a red light after a full stop, and if you are in the far left lane of a one-way street, you may turn left into the adjacent left lane of a one-way street at a red light after a full stop. Everyone in a moving vehicle is required to wear a seat belt.

BY TAXI

Because most everything in Portland is fairly close, getting around by taxi can be economical. Although there are almost always taxis waiting in line at major hotels, you won't find them cruising the streets—you'll have to phone for one. **Broadway Cab** (② 503/227-1234) and **Radio Cab** (② 503/227-1212) charge $2.50 for the first mile, $2 for each additional mile, and $1 for additional passengers.

ON FOOT

City blocks in Portland are about half the size of most city blocks elsewhere, and the entire downtown area covers only about 13 blocks by 26 blocks. This makes Portland a very easy place to explore on foot. The city has been very active in encouraging people to get out of their cars and onto the sidewalks downtown. The sidewalks are wide and there are many fountains, works of art, and small parks with benches.

FAST FACTS: Portland

AAA The **American Automobile Association** (② 800/222-4357; www.aaaorid.com) has a Portland office at 600 SW Market St. (② 503/222-6734) that offers free city maps to members.

Airport See "Getting There" in chapter 2 and "Arriving," in section 1 of this chapter.

American Express **Azumano Travel,** 400 SW Stark St. (② 800/777-2018 or 503/294-2000), is an **American Express Travel Services Representative.** For cardmember services, phone ② 800/528-4800. Call ② 800/AXP-TRIP or go to **www.american express.com** for other locations or general information.

Area Codes The Portland metro area has two area codes—503 and 971—and it is necessary to dial all 10 digits of a telephone number, even when making local calls.

Babysitters If your hotel doesn't offer babysitting services, call **Northwest Nannies** (② 503/245-5288).

Car Rentals See section 2, "Getting Around," earlier in this chapter.

Climate See section 4, "When to Go," in chapter 2.

Dentist Contact the **Multnomah Dental Society** (② 503/513-5010) for a referral.

Doctor If you need a physician referral while in Portland, contact the **Medical Society of Metropolitan Portland** (② 503/222-0156).

Emergencies For police, fire, or medical emergencies, phone ② 911.

Eyeglass Repair Check out **Binyon's Master Eye Associates,** 803 SW Morrison St. (© **503/226-6688**).

Hospitals Three conveniently located area hospitals are **Legacy Good Samaritan,** 1015 NW 22nd Ave. (© **503/413-7711**); **Providence Portland Medical Center,** 4805 NE Glisan St. (© **503/215-1111**); and the **Oregon Health & Sciences University Hospital,** 3181 SW Sam Jackson Park Rd. (© **503/494-8311**), which is just southwest of the city center and has a drop-in clinic.

Information See "Visitor Information," in section 1 of this chapter.

Internet Access If you need to check e-mail while you're in Portland, first check with your hotel or, if you have your own laptop with Wi-Fi, find a cafe with wireless access. Otherwise, visit a **FedEx Kinko's.** There's one downtown at 221 SW Alder St. (© **503/224-6550**) and northwest at 950 NW 23rd Ave. (© **503/222-4133**). You can also try the **Multnomah County Library,** 801 SW 10th Ave. (© **503/988-5123**), which is Portland's main library and offers online services.

Liquor Laws The legal minimum drinking age in Oregon is 21. Aside from on-premises sales of cocktails in bars and restaurants, hard liquor can be purchased only in liquor stores. Beer and wine are available in convenience stores and grocery stores. Brewpubs tend to sell only beer and wine, but some also have licenses to sell hard liquor.

Maps See "City Layout," in section 1 of this chapter.

Newspapers & Magazines Portland's morning daily newspaper is *The Oregonian.* For arts and entertainment information and listings, consult the "A&E" section of the Friday *Oregonian* or pick up a free copy of *Willamette Week* at Powell's Books and other bookstores, convenience stores, or cafes.

Pharmacies Convenient to most downtown hotels, **Central Drug,** 538 SW Fourth Ave. (© **503/226-2222**), is open Monday through Friday from 9am to 6pm, Saturday from 10am to 4pm.

Photographic Needs **Wolf Camera,** 220 SW Main St. (© **503/224-2365**), offers 1-hour film processing. **Camera World,** 400 SW Sixth Ave. (© **503/241-7979**), is the largest camera and video store in the city.

Police To reach the police, call © **911.**

Post Offices The most convenient downtown post office is University Station, 1505 SW Sixth Ave. (© **503/274-1362**), open Monday through Friday from 7am to 6pm, Saturday from 10am to 3pm. For more information, call ℂ **800/275-8777**.

Restrooms There are public restrooms underneath Starbucks coffee shop in Pioneer Courthouse Square, in downtown shopping malls, and in hotel lobbies.

Safety Because of its relatively small size and progressive emphasis on keeping the downtown alive and growing, Portland is still a relatively safe city. Take extra precautions, however, if you venture into the entertainment district along West Burnside Street and in Chinatown at night. If you plan to go hiking in Forest Park, don't leave anything valuable in your car. This holds true in the Skidmore Historic District (Old Town) as well.

Smoking Although many of the restaurants listed in this book are smoke-free, many Portland restaurants allow smoking. At most high-end restaurants, the smoking area is usually in the bar/lounge, and although many restaurants have separate bar menus, most will serve you off the regular menu even if you are eating in the bar. There are a few nonsmoking bars in Portland.

Taxes Portland is a shopper's paradise—there's no sales tax. However, there is a 12.5% tax on hotel rooms within the city and a 12.5% tax on car rentals (plus an additional airport-use fee if you pick up your rental car at the airport; this additional fee is anywhere from around 10% to around 16%). Outside the city, the room tax varies.

Taxis See section 2, "Getting Around," earlier in this chapter.

Time Zone Portland is on Pacific Time, 3 hours behind the East Coast. In the summer, daylight saving time is observed and clocks are set forward 1 hour.

Transit Info For bus, MAX, and Portland Streetcar information, call the **TriMet Customer Assistance Office** (ℂ **503/238-7433**).

Weather If it's summer, it's sunny; otherwise, there's a chance of rain. This almost always suffices, but for specifics, call the Portland Oregon Visitor Association's **weather information hot line** (ℂ **503/275-9792**). If you want to know how to pack before you arrive, check **www.cnn.com/weather** or **www.weather.com**.

4

Where to Stay

Whether you're looking for a downtown corporate high-rise, a restored historic hotel, a hip boutique hotel, a romantic B&B, or just something relatively inexpensive, you'll find it in Portland. You even have a couple of good choices for riverfront hotels.

If your budget won't allow for a first-class downtown business hotel, try near the airport or elsewhere on the outskirts of the city (Troutdale and Gresham on the east side; Beaverton and Hillsboro on the west; Wilsonville and Lake Oswego in the south; and Vancouver, Washington, in the north), where you're more likely to find inexpensive to moderately priced motels.

You'll find the greatest concentration of bed-and-breakfasts in the Irvington neighborhood of northeast Portland. This area is close to downtown and is generally quite convenient even if you are here on business.

In the following listings, price categories are based on the rate for a double room in high season. (Most hotels charge the same for a single or double room.) Keep in mind that the rates listed do not include local room taxes, which vary between 7% and 11.5%.

For comparison purposes, we list what hotels call "rack rates," or walk-in rates—but you should never have to pay these highly inflated prices. Various discounts (AAA, senior, corporate, and Entertainment Book) often reduce these rates, so be sure to ask (and check each hotel's website for Internet specials). In fact, you can often get a discounted corporate rate simply by flashing a business card (your own, that is). At inexpensive chain motels, there are almost always discounted rates for AAA members and seniors.

You'll also find that room rates are almost always considerably lower October through April (the rainy season), and large downtown hotels often offer weekend discounts of up to 50% throughout the year. Some of the large, upscale hotel chains have now gone to an airline-type rate system based on occupancy, so if you call early enough, before a hotel books up, you might get a really good rate. On the other hand, call at the last minute and you might catch a

Where to Stay in Portland

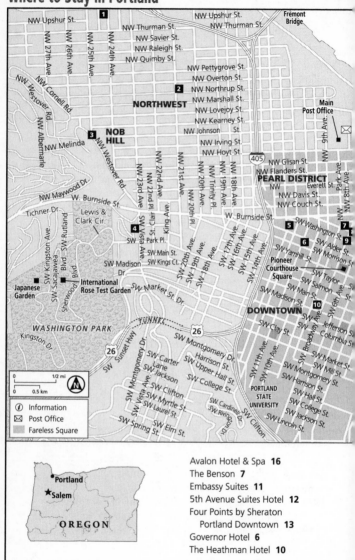

Avalon Hotel & Spa **16**
The Benson **7**
Embassy Suites **11**
5th Avenue Suites Hotel **12**
Four Points by Sheraton
   Portland Downtown **13**
Governor Hotel **6**
The Heathman Hotel **10**

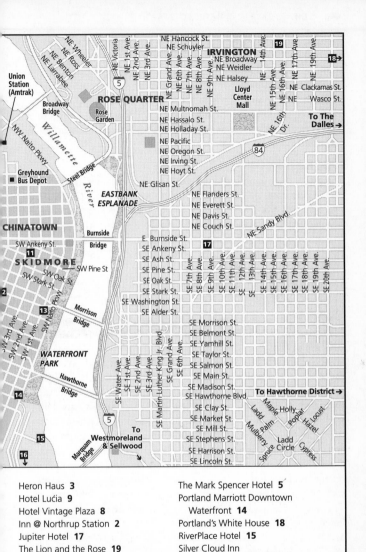

Heron Haus **3**
Hotel Lućia **9**
Hotel Vintage Plaza **8**
Inn @ Northrup Station **2**
Jupiter Hotel **17**
The Lion and the Rose **19**
MacMaster House Bed
   and Breakfast Inn **4**

The Mark Spencer Hotel **5**
Portland Marriott Downtown
   Waterfront **14**
Portland's White House **18**
RiverPlace Hotel **15**
Silver Cloud Inn
   Portland Downtown **1**

cancellation and still be offered a low rate. However, it's always advisable to make reservations as far in advance as possible if you're planning to visit during the busy summer months. Also be sure to ask about special packages (romance, golf, or theater), which most of the more expensive hotels usually offer.

Most hotels offer nonsmoking rooms, and most bed-and-breakfasts are exclusively nonsmoking. Most hotels also offer wheelchair-accessible rooms.

HELPING HANDS

If you're having trouble booking a room, try the **Portland Oregon Visitors Association (POVA),** 701 SW Sixth Ave., Portland, OR 97205 (© **877/678-5263** or 503/275-8355; www.travelportland.com), which offers a reservation service for the Portland metro area.

For information on **bed-and-breakfasts** in the Portland area, call the **Portland Oregon Visitors Association** (© **877/678-5263** or 503/275-8355; www.travelportland.com). Also try contacting the **Oregon Bed and Breakfast Guild,** P.O. Box 3187, Ashland, OR 97520 (© **800/944-6196;** www.obbg.org).

1 Downtown

EXPENSIVE

Avalon Hotel & Spa 👍👍👍   This hotel sits right on the banks of the Willamette River just south of downtown. Although this location is a bit inconvenient for exploring the city on foot, there is a riverside bike path right in front of the hotel, making this a good bet if you're a jogger or like to take leisurely walks. The Avalon's contemporary decor makes it one of the most stylish hotels in the city, and the riverfront rooms, most of which have balconies, provide good views and a chance to breathe in fresh air while soaking up life on the Willamette. The hotel's stylish restaurant boasts the same great river views and walls of glass to make the most of the setting. The full-service spa just off the lobby gives this luxurious boutique hotel the feel of a much larger resort.

0455 SW Hamilton Court, Portland, OR 97239. © **888/556-4402** or 503/802-5800. Fax 503/802-5820. www.avalonhotelandspa.com. 99 units. $155–$215 double; $285–$650 suite. Children under 18 stay free in parent's room. AE, DC, DISC, MC, V. Valet parking $10. **Amenities:** Restaurant (New American); lounge; health club; day spa; Jacuzzi; sauna; concierge; courtesy car; business center; 24-hr. room service; massage; laundry service; dry cleaning. *In room:* A/C, TV, dataport, coffeemaker, hair dryer, iron, safe, high-speed Internet access, Wi-Fi.

5th Avenue Suites Hotel 𝄐𝄐   Located a block from Pioneer Courthouse Square and within a few blocks of the best downtown shopping, this unpretentious yet sophisticated hotel is housed in what was originally a department store. Artwork by Northwest artists fills the lobby, and in the afternoon there are complimentary tastings of Oregon and Washington wines. Guest rooms, most of which are suites, are way over-the-top when it comes to decor— striped wallpaper, big padded headboards on the beds, red couches. In other words, colors and patterns everywhere, but it all comes together in a pleasantly theatrical fashion that makes these some of my favorite rooms in Portland. Plus, bathrooms have lots of counter space. In the suites, sliding French doors with curtains divide the living room from the bedrooms but don't provide much privacy. The hotel's **Red Star Roast House** serves upscale comfort food.

506 SW Washington St., Portland, OR 97204. © **888/207-2201** or 503/222-0001. Fax 503/222-0004. www.5thavenuesuites.com. 221 units. $139–$195 double; $159–$325 suite. Children under age 18 stay free in parent's room. AE, DC, DISC, MC, V. Valet parking $25. Pets accepted. **Amenities:** Restaurant (American); lounge; exercise room; access to nearby health club; Aveda day spa; concierge; business center; 24-hr. room service; massage; laundry service; dry cleaning. *In room:* A/C, TV, dataport, minibar, coffeemaker, hair dryer, iron, Wi-Fi.

Governor Hotel 𝄐𝄐𝄐   This plush historic hotel is located right on the Portland Streetcar line in downtown and has a very classic and masculine feel about it. The huge lobby abounds in marble and has gilded plasterwork ceilings reminiscent of the royal palaces of Europe. Guest room furnishing have much cleaner lines, with vaguely Art Deco styling. Guest rooms vary considerably in size but are all attractively decorated. The least expensive rooms are rather small but are nevertheless very comfortable. Still, I'd opt for one of the deluxe guest rooms. Unfortunately, bathrooms are, in general, quite cramped by today's standards and lack counter space. Suites, on the other hand, are spacious, and some even have huge patios overlooking the city. Be sure to check out the hotel's restaurant—Jake's Grill—which has a beautiful mural commemorating the Lewis and Clark expedition.

614 SW 11th Ave., Portland, OR 97205. © **800/554-3456** or 503/224-3400. Fax 503/241-2122. www.govhotel.com. 100 units. $169–$189 double; $239–$500 suite. AE, DC, DISC, MC, V. Valet parking $21. **Amenities:** Restaurant (American); lounge; concierge; business center; 24-hr. room service; massage; laundry service; dry cleaning. *In room:* A/C, TV, dataport, minibar, coffeemaker, hair dryer, iron, safe, high-speed Internet access, Wi-Fi.

The Heathman Hotel 𝄐𝄐   The Heathman has long been considered one of Portland's top hotels, but in many ways this hotel suffers from an identity crisis. An incongruous beefeater doorman ushers guests into a minimalist lobby that is adjacent to an utterly traditional "tea court," which itself is adjacent to the hotel's French restaurant, which is owned by the McCormick and Schmick's restaurant chain and is decorated with Andy Warhol prints. Guest rooms, all recently redecorated, are theatrically decorated in a vaguely Art Deco motif that seems cluttered. All the tabletop amenities and abundant pillows tend to make the rooms feel even smaller than they actually are, and the basic rooms are definitely small. If you decide to give this place a try, you'll get to choose your bed—feather bed, pillow-top, or Tempur-Pedic.

1001 SW Broadway, Portland, OR 97205. (℃) **800/551-0011** or 503/241-4100. Fax 503/790-7110. www.heathmanhotel.com. 150 units. $199–$249 double; $249–$1,000 suite. Children 12 and under stay free in parent's room. AE, DC, DISC, MC, V. Parking $26. Pets accepted ($25). **Amenities:** Restaurant (French/Northwest); lounge; exercise room and access to nearby health club; concierge; 24-hr. room service; laundry service; dry cleaning. *In room:* A/C, TV, dataport, minibar, French-press coffeemaker, hair dryer, iron, high-speed Internet access.

Hotel Lućia 🎭🎭   Portland may not have a W Hotel, but it does have the Lućia, which is just as hip. Located across from the prestigious and very traditional Benson hotel, the Lućia is the Portland address of choice for young business travelers with a taste for contemporary style. There's a big emphasis on the visual arts here, with paintings by Northwest artists on the lobby walls, and black-and-white photos by famed White House photographer David Hume Kennerly throughout the hotel. Guest rooms are some of the prettiest in the city, with great beds and bathrooms that have lots of chrome and frosted-glass counters. Drawbacks here include paper-thin walls in some rooms, a young and inexperienced staff, and a slow elevator (despite the stylish makeover, this is an old building). Try to get a discounted rate to make up for these shortcomings.

400 SW Broadway, Portland, OR 97205. (℃) **877/225-1717** or 503/225-1717. Fax 503/225-1919. www.hotellucia.com. 128 units. $149–$255 double; $265–$625 suite. Children under 18 stay free in parent's room. AE, DC, DISC, MC, V. Parking $23. **Amenities:** Restaurant (Thai); lounge; exercise room; concierge; business center; 24-hr. room service; laundry service; dry cleaning. *In room:* A/C, TV, dataport, minibar, hair dryer, iron, safe, Wi-Fi.

Hotel Vintage Plaza 🎭🎭   This hotel, which was built in 1894 and is on the National Register of Historic Places, is *the* place to stay in Portland if you are a wine lover. A wine theme predominates in the hotel's decor, and there are complimentary evening tastings of Northwest wines. There are a wide variety of room types here, and though the standard rooms are worth recommending, the starlight rooms and bi-level suites are the real scene-stealers. The starlight rooms in particular are truly extraordinary. Though small, they have greenhouse-style windows that provide very romantic views at night and let in floods of light during the day. The bi-level suites, some with Japanese soaking tubs, are equally attractive spaces. **Pazzo Ristorante** is a dark, intimate trattoria.

422 SW Broadway, Portland, OR 97205. ⓒ **800/243-0555** or 503/228-1212. Fax 503/228-3598. www.vintageplaza.com. 107 units. $129–$259 double; $149–$399 suite. Children under 18 stay free in parent's room. AE, DC, DISC, MC, V. Valet parking $25. Pets accepted. **Amenities:** Restaurant (Italian); lounge; exercise room; access to nearby health club; concierge; business center; 24-hr. room service; massage; laundry service; dry cleaning. *In room:* A/C, TV, dataport, minibar, fridge, coffeemaker, hair dryer, iron, high-speed Internet access, Wi-Fi.

Portland Marriott Downtown Waterfront 🎀🎀   Located just across Waterfront Park and Naito Parkway from the Willamette River, the high-rise Portland Marriott offers great views of Mount Hood from its upper east-side rooms, and this alone would be reason enough to stay here. That the park across the street serves as the site of virtually all of Portland's main festivals also makes it a good choice if you're in town for one of these festivals. (If you're planning a weekend visit, be sure to find out if there's a festival scheduled; depending on your interest in the event, you might have a great seat for the show or suffer from the noise and crowds.) Otherwise, this standard corporate high-rise doesn't have a whole lot of character, though there is a nice Japanese-style garden outside the front door. Most of the guest rooms have small balconies.

1401 SW Naito Pkwy., Portland, OR 97201. ⓒ **800/228-9290** or 503/226-7600. Fax 503/221-1789. www.marriott.com/pdxor. 503 units. $109–$259 double; $400–$600 suite. Children under 12 stay free in parent's room. AE, DC, DISC, MC, V. Valet parking $23. **Amenities:** 2 restaurants (American); 2 lounges; indoor pool; exercise room; access to nearby health club; Jacuzzi; concierge; business center; room service; coin-op laundry; laundry service; dry cleaning; concierge level. *In room:* A/C, TV, dataport, coffeemaker, hair dryer, iron, high-speed Internet access.

RiverPlace Hotel 🎀🎀🎀   With the Willamette River at its back doorstep and the sloping lawns of Waterfront Park to one side, the RiverPlace is Portland's only downtown waterfront hotel. This alone would be enough to recommend the hotel, but its quiet boutique-hotel atmosphere would make it an excellent choice even if it weren't on the water. In general, furnishings are neither as elegant nor as luxurious as at The Benson, but more than half the rooms are suites, some of which have wood-burning fireplaces and whirlpool baths.

There are also condominiums for long stays; however, the river-view standard king rooms here are the hotel's best deal. The hotel's restaurant overlooks the river, and there's also a comfortable bar with a patio overlooking the river. All in all, what you're paying for here is the waterfront locale, which is fine by me.

1510 SW Harbor Way, Portland, OR 97201. ✆ **800/227-1333** or 503/228-3233. Fax 503/295-6161. www.riverplacehotel.com. 84 units. $169–$219 double; $169–$219 junior suite; $199 and up for a suite. AE, DC, DISC, MC, V. Valet parking $23. Pets accepted ($45 nonrefundable cleaning fee). **Amenities:** Restaurant (Northwest); lounge; access to nearby health club; day spa; Jacuzzi; sauna; concierge; business center; 24-hr. room service; massage; laundry service; dry cleaning. *In room:* A/C, TV/DVD, dataport, fridge, hair dryer, iron, Wi-Fi.

MODERATE

The Benson 𝔊𝔊𝔊   Built in 1912, The Benson exudes old-world sophistication and elegance. In the French baroque lobby, walnut paneling frames a marble fireplace, Austrian crystal chandeliers hang from the ornate plasterwork ceiling, and a marble staircase allows for grand entrances. These are the poshest digs in Portland, and guest rooms are luxuriously furnished in a plush Euro-luxe styling. Rooms vary considerably in size, and most of the deluxe kings are particularly spacious. However, the corner junior suites, which are large and have lots of windows, are the hotel's best deal. All the guest rooms have Tempur-Pedic mattresses. Bathrooms, unfortunately, are small and have little shelf space. The hotel's **London Grill** is well known for its Sunday brunch. Just off the lobby, there's El Gaucho steakhouse; in the Lobby Bar, there's live jazz in the evenings.

309 SW Broadway, Portland, OR 97205. ✆ **888/523-6766** or 503/228-2000. Fax 503/471-3920. www.bensonhotel.com. 287 units. $124–$229 double; $199–$299 junior suite; $400–$1,000 suite. Children under 18 stay free in parent's room. AE, DC, DISC, MC, V. Valet parking $25. Pets accepted ($75). **Amenities:** 2 restaurants (Northwest/Continental, steaks); lounge; exercise room; access to nearby health club; concierge; business center; 24-hr. room service; babysitting; laundry service; dry cleaning. *In room:* A/C, TV, dataport, minibar, coffeemaker, hair dryer, iron, Wi-Fi.

Embassy Suites 𝔊𝔊 *(Kids* *(Value*   Located in the restored former Multnomah Hotel, which originally opened in 1912, the Embassy Suites has a beautiful large lobby that is a masterpiece of gilded plasterwork. The accommodations here are primarily two-room suites, with the exception of a handful of studio suites. In keeping with the historic nature of the hotel, the suites have classically styled furnishings. However, what's much more important is that they give you lots of room to spread out, a rarity in downtown hotels. The hotel's Portland Steak and Chophouse has a classic dark and woody steakhouse decor and a large bar. There's a nightly complimentary evening manager's reception.

319 SW Pine St., Portland, OR 97204. *© **800/EMBASSY*** or 503/279-9000. Fax 503/497-9051. www.embassyportland.com. 276 units. $139–$209 double. Rates include full breakfast. Children 18 and under stay free in parent's room. AE, DC, DISC, MC, V. Valet parking $22; self-parking $15. **Amenities:** Restaurant (steak); lounge; indoor pool; exercise room; access to nearby health club; day spa; Jacuzzi; sauna; concierge; car-rental desk; courtesy van; business center; room service; massage; babysitting; laundry service; dry cleaning. *In room:* A/C, TV, dataport, fridge, coffeemaker, hair dryer, iron, Wi-Fi.

Four Points by Sheraton Portland Downtown ☆☆ *Value*
Overlooking Waterfront Park and located on the MAX light-rail line, this 1960s vintage hotel is nondescript from the outside, but the inside has a contemporary look that makes it surprisingly stylish for a budget hotel. You are only steps from the Willamette River (although not actually on the water) and are also close to businesses, fine restaurants, and shopping. Guest rooms are comfortable and have a modern styling.

50 SW Morrison St., Portland, OR 97204-3390. *© **800/368-7764*** or 503/221-0711. Fax 503/274-0312. www.fourpoints.com/portlanddowntown. 140 units. $99–$150 double. AE, DC, DISC, MC, V. Parking $11. Pets accepted. **Amenities:** Restaurant (American/international); lounge; exercise room; access to nearby health club; business center; room service; dry cleaning. *In room:* A/C, TV, dataport, coffeemaker, hair dryer, iron, high-speed Internet access, Wi-Fi.

The Mark Spencer Hotel ☆ *Value*   This economically priced
downtown hotel just off West Burnside Street is ideally situated just around the corner from both Powell's City of Books and Jake's Famous Crawfish, one of Portland's oldest and most popular restaurants. The trendy Pearl District begins only a couple of blocks from the hotel, and the Portland Streetcar stops nearby. The rooms and suites here are a bit dated in their decor, but all have kitchenettes. When you've had enough of wandering the city streets, head up to the hotel's rooftop garden deck for a different perspective on Portland. The Mark Spencer is a favorite of touring Broadway shows when they're in town.

409 SW 11th Ave., Portland, OR 97205. *© **800/548-3934*** or 503/224-3293. Fax 503/223-7848. www.markspencer.com. 101 units. $59–$129 double; $79–$169 suite. Rates include continental breakfast. Children under 12 stay free in parent's room. AE, DC, DISC, MC, V. Parking $15. Pets accepted ($10 per day). **Amenities:** Access to nearby health club; concierge; coin-op laundry; laundry service; dry cleaning. *In room:* A/C, TV, dataport, kitchen, fridge, coffeemaker, hair dryer, iron, safe, high-speed Internet access, Wi-Fi.

2 Nob Hill & Northwest Portland

EXPENSIVE

Heron Haus 🏨🏨 A short walk from the bustling Nob Hill shopping and dining district of northwest Portland, the Heron Haus B&B offers outstanding accommodations, spectacular views, and tranquil surroundings. Surprisingly, the house still features some of the original plumbing. In most places this would be a liability, but not here, since the same man who plumbed Portland's famous Pittock Mansion (p. 88) did the plumbing here. Many of that building's unusual bathroom features are also found at the Heron Haus—one shower has *seven* showerheads. In another room there's a modern whirlpool spa with excellent views of the city. All the rooms have fireplaces.

2545 NW Westover Rd., Portland, OR 97210. ⓒ **503/274-1846.** Fax 503/248-4055. www.heronhaus.com. 6 units. $135–$350 double. Rates include continental breakfast. MC, V. Free parking. *In room:* A/C, TV, dataport, hair dryer, iron, high-speed Internet access.

MODERATE

Inn @ Northrup Station 🏨🏨 *Finds* Colorful, hip, retro. That about sums up this hotel in the trendy Nob Hill neighborhood. On top of this high style, the hotel has large rooms with kitchens or kitchenettes, and the Portland Streetcar stops right outside the hotel, which makes this a convenient hotel for exploring the city's most interesting neighborhoods. The colorful retro decor really sets this all-suite hotel apart from more cookie-cutter corporate hotels around town, and if you appreciate bright colors and contemporary styling, this should be your first choice in town. Lots of the rooms here have balconies, and there's a rooftop terrace. The hotel's location in a quiet residential neighborhood is another plus, and several of Portland's top restaurants are within a short walk.

2025 NW Northrup St., Portland, OR 97209. ⓒ **800/224-1180** or 503/224-0543. Fax 503/273-2102. www.northrupstation.com. 70 units. $99–$199 double. Rates include continental breakfast. Children under 12 stay free in parent's room. AE, DC, DISC, MC, V. Free parking. **Amenities:** Laundry service; dry cleaning. *In room:* A/C TV, dataport, fridge, coffeemaker, hair dryer, Wi-Fi.

MacMaster House Bed and Breakfast Inn 🏨 Located close to both Washington Park and the trendy shops and restaurants of the Nob Hill neighborhood, this imposing mansion sits high above the street and is surrounded by huge old rhododendrons that are gorgeous in the spring. Many of the guest rooms have interesting murals on the walls, and four rooms have fireplaces. One of the fireplace

(Kids) Family-Friendly Hotels

Embassy Suites (p. 48)   Located in the center of the city, this renovated historic hotel offers spacious rooms (mostly two-room suites). You and the kids will have room to spread out and can hang out by the indoor pool when you tire of exploring Portland.

Homewood Suites by Hilton Vancouver/Portland (p. 54) Although this hotel is across the Columbia River in Vancouver, Washington, its location right across the street from the river, a paved riverside trail, a fun family restaurant, and a brewpub all add up to convenience for families. That you'll get a one- or two-bedroom apartment with a full kitchen just makes life on vacation that much easier.

The Lakeshore Inn (p. 56)   This reasonably priced inn is right on the shore of the lake and it also has a pool. The big rooms with kitchenettes are great for families; for more space, opt for a one- or two-bedroom suite.

rooms also has a claw-foot tub. Some of the rooms are on the third floor, and the inn itself is up a flight of stairs from the street, so you need to be in good shape to stay here.

1041 SW Vista Ave., Portland, OR 97205. © 800/774-9523 or 503/223-7362. www.macmaster.com. 7 units (5 with shared bathroom). $99–$129 double with shared bathroom; $155–$169 suite. Rates include full breakfast. Children 14 and older welcome. AE, MC, V. *In room:* No phone, Wi-Fi.

Silver Cloud Inn Portland Downtown ♠   This hotel is on the edge of Portland's trendy Nob Hill neighborhood, and though it's also on the edge of an industrial area, it is still a very attractive and comfortable place (ask for a room away from Vaughn St.). Reasonable rates are the main draw here, but the rooms are also well designed. The minisuites have wet bars, microwave ovens, and separate seating areas, but the king minisuites with whirlpool tubs are my favorites. The best thing about the hotel is its location within a 5-minute drive (or 15-min. walk) of a half-dozen of the city's best restaurants. To find the hotel, take I-405 to Ore. 30 west and get off at the Vaughn Street exit.

2426 NW Vaughn St., Portland, OR 97210. © 800/205-6939 or 503/242-2400. Fax 503/242-1770. www.silvercloud.com. 82 units. $99–$139 double. Rates include continental breakfast. Children under 18 stay free in parent's room. AE, DC, DISC,

MC, V. Free parking. **Amenities:** Exercise room; business center; guest laundry; laundry service; dry cleaning. *In room:* A/C, TV, dataport, coffeemaker, hair dryer, iron, free local calls, high-speed Internet access.

3 The Rose Quarter & Irvington

EXPENSIVE

The Lion and the Rose 🐾🐾   This imposing Queen Anne–style Victorian inn is located in the Irvington District, a fairly quiet residential neighborhood 1 block off Northeast Broadway. It's a good choice if you want to keep your driving to a minimum. Restaurants, cafes, eclectic boutiques, and a huge shopping mall are all within 4 blocks. Even without the splendid location, the inn would be a gem. Each guest room has a distinctively different decor. In the Lavonna Room, there are bright colors and a turret sitting area, while in the deep green Starina Room you'll find an imposing Edwardian bed and armoire. The Garden Room and the Lavonna Room bathrooms have claw-foot tubs, while some rooms have rather cramped, though attractive, bathrooms. If you have problems climbing stairs, ask for the ground floor's Rose Room, which has a whirlpool tub. Breakfasts are sumptuous affairs, great for lingering.

1810 NE 15th Ave., Portland, OR 97212. © 800/955-1647 or 503/287-9245. Fax 503/287-9247. www.lionrose.com. 6 units. $120–$175 double. AE, DISC, MC, V. Children 10 and older welcome. **Amenities:** Concierge. *In room:* A/C, TV, dataport, hair dryer, iron, free local calls, Wi-Fi.

MODERATE

Portland's White House 🐾🐾   With massive columns framing the entrance, semicircular driveway, and in the front garden a bubbling fountain, this imposing Greek-revival mansion bears a more than passing resemblance to its namesake in Washington, D.C. Behind the mahogany front doors, a huge entrance hall with original hand-painted wall murals is flanked by a parlor and the formal dining room, where the large breakfast is served beneath sparkling crystal chandeliers. A double staircase leads past a large stained-glass window to the second-floor accommodations. Canopy and brass queen-size beds, antique furnishings, and bathrooms with claw-foot tubs further the feeling of classic luxury here. Request the balcony room, and you can gaze out past the Greek columns and imagine you're in the Oval Office. There are also three rooms in the restored carriage house.

1914 NE 22nd Ave., Portland, OR 97212. © 800/272-7131 or 503/287-7131. Fax 503/249-1641. www.portlandswhitehouse.com. 8 units. $125–$225 double. Rates include full breakfast. AE, DISC, MC, V. *In room:* A/C, TV, dataport, Wi-Fi.

INEXPENSIVE

Jupiter Hotel 🦋 *(Finds)*   Although this place calls itself a boutique hotel, it's actually a boutique motel. However, this motel has had an extreme makeover and is now an über-hip address for the Portland arts crowd and those in town to participate in the city's hip scene. With its glowing blue exterior wall panels, piped-in music in the courtyard, and log-cabin swank Doug Fir Lounge, the Jupiter has enough going on to keep the party going all night long, so don't plan on getting much sleep if you stay here. Platform beds, fuzzy pillows, photo-murals on the walls, retro accents, and dim lighting (or is it supposed to be romantic lighting?) provide guest rooms with plenty of retro-hip styling for young travelers on a tight budget.

800 E. Burnside, Portland, OR 97214. ✆ **877/800-0004** or 503/230-9200. www.jupiter hotel.com. 80 units. $89–$99 double. AE, DISC, MC, V. **Amenities:** Restaurant (New American); lounge; massage. *In room:* A/C, TV, dataport, hair dryer, Wi-Fi.

McMenamins Kennedy School 🦋 *(Finds)*   The Kennedy School, which was an elementary school from 1915 to 1975, is owned by the same folks who turned Portland's old poor farm into the most entertaining and unusual B&B in the state (see the listing for McMenamins Edgefield, below). In the guest rooms you'll still find the original blackboards and great big school clocks (you know, like the one you used to watch so expectantly). However, the classroom/guest rooms here now have their own bathrooms, so you won't have to raise your hand or walk down the hall. On the premises you'll also find a restaurant, a beer garden, a movie theater pub, a cigar bar, and a big hot soaking pool. The Kennedy School is located well north of stylish Irvington neighborhood in an up-and-coming part of the city that dates from the early years of the 20th century.

5736 NE 33rd Ave., Portland, OR 97211. ✆ **888/249-3983** or 503/249-3983. www. mcmenamins.com. 35 units. $84–$99 double. Children 6 and under stay free. AE, DC, DISC, MC, V. **Amenities:** Restaurant (American); 4 lounges; soaking pool; massage. *In room:* Wi-Fi.

4 Vancouver, Washington

Located just across the Columbia River from Portland, Vancouver, Washington, is an economical nearby area from which to explore the Portland area.

MODERATE

The Heathman Lodge 🦋🦋 *(Value)*   Mountain lodge meets urban chic at this suburban Vancouver hotel adjacent to the Vancouver Mall. Located 20 minutes by car from downtown Portland, the hotel is well placed for exploring both the Columbia Gorge and Mount St. Helens. With its log, stone, and cedar-shingle construction, this hotel conjures up the Northwest's historic mountain lodges. As at Timberline Lodge on Oregon's Mount Hood, this hotel is filled with artwork and embellished with rugged Northwest-inspired craftswork, including totem poles, Eskimo kayak frames, and Pendleton blankets. Guest rooms feature a mix of rustic pine and peeled-hickory furniture as well as rawhide lampshades and Pendleton-inspired bedspreads. Most rooms also have Tempur-Pedic mattresses.

7801 NE Greenwood Dr., Vancouver, WA 98662. (© **888/475-3100** or 360/254-3100. Fax 360/254-6100. www.heathmanlodge.com. 142 units. $79–$149 double; from $159–$350 suite. AE, DC, DISC, MC, V. **Amenities:** Restaurant (Northwest); lounge; indoor pool; exercise room; Jacuzzi; sauna; concierge; business center; room service; guest laundry; laundry service; dry cleaning. *In room:* A/C, TV, dataport, fridge, coffeemaker, hair dryer, iron, Wi-Fi.

Homewood Suites by Hilton Vancouver/Portland &* (Kids
Located across the street from the Columbia River, this modern suburban all-suite hotel is a great choice for families. The hotel charges surprisingly reasonable rates for large apartment-like accommodations that include full kitchens. Rates include not only a large breakfast, but afternoon snacks as well (Mon–Thurs). These snacks are substantial enough to pass for dinner if you aren't too hungry. The hotel is right across the street from both a beach-theme restaurant and a brewpub. Across the street, you'll also find a paved riverside path that's great for walking or jogging. The only drawback is that it's a 15- to 20-minute drive to downtown Portland.

701 SE Columbia Shores Blvd., Vancouver, WA 98661. (© **800/CALL-HOME** or 360/750-1100. Fax 360/750-4899. www.homewoodsuites.com. 104 units. $99–$179 double. Rates include full breakfast. AE, DC, DISC, MC, V. Free parking. Pets accepted ($25 first day, $10 subsequent days). **Amenities:** Outdoor pool; exercise room; Jacuzzi; sports court; business center; coin-op laundry; laundry service; dry cleaning. *In room:* A/C, TV, dataport, kitchen, fridge, coffeemaker, hair dryer, iron, free local calls, high-speed Internet access.

5 The Airport Area & Troutdale

There are lots of moderately priced hotels in the airport area, which makes this a good place to look for a room if you arrive with no reservation.

MODERATE
Embassy Suites at Portland Airport &* (Kids   There are few travel experiences worse than arriving after dark in a city you've

never been to and having to search for your hotel. If you'll be arriving at Portland International Airport at night, you'll have no problem finding this hotel: It's the first hotel you come to as you exit the airport grounds. As at other Embassy Suites, you'll get a spacious two-room suite that opens onto a large atrium complete with waterfalls and fish ponds. Because these suites are so large, the hotel is a good choice for families.

7900 NE 82nd Ave., Portland, OR 97220. (C) **800/EMBASSY** or 503/460-3000. Fax 502/460-3030. www.embassysuites.com. 251 units. $109–$219 double. Rates include full breakfast. Children under 18 stay free in parent's room. AE, DC, DISC, MC, V. Free parking. **Amenities:** Restaurant (American); indoor pool; exercise room; Jacuzzi; sauna; courtesy airport shuttle; business center; room service; coin-op laundry; dry cleaning. *In room:* A/C, TV, dataport, fridge, coffeemaker, microwave, hair dryer, iron, high-speed Internet access.

McMenamins Edgefield ⭑ *(Finds)* Ideally situated for exploring the Columbia Gorge and Mount Hood, this flagship of the McMenamin microbrewery empire is the former Multnomah County poor farm. Today the property includes not only tastefully decorated guest rooms with antique furnishings, but a brewery, a pub, a beer garden, a restaurant, a movie theater, a winery, a wine-tasting room, a distillery, a golf course, a cigar bar in an old shed, and extensive gardens. With so much in one spot, this makes a great base for exploring the area. The beautiful grounds give this inn the feel of a remote retreat, though you are still within 30 miles of Portland.

2126 SW Halsey St., Troutdale, OR 97060. (C) **800/669-8610** or 503/669-8610. Fax 503/492-7750. www.mcmenamins.com. 114 units (100 with shared bathroom). $50–$90 double with shared bathroom; $95–$115 double with private bathroom; $30 hostel bed per person. Children under 7 stay free in parent's room. AE, DC, DISC, MC, V. **Amenities:** 3 restaurants (Northwest, American); 6 lounges; 18-hole par-3 golf course; business center; massage. *In room:* No phone, Wi-Fi.

Silver Cloud Inn Portland Airport ⭑ *(Value)* Conveniently located right outside the airport, this hotel has one of the best backyards of any hotel in the Portland area. A lake, lawns, and trees create a tranquil setting despite the proximity of both the airport and a busy nearby road. Rooms are designed primarily for business travelers, but even if you aren't here on an expense account, they are a good value, especially those with whirlpool tubs. Some suites have gas fireplaces. Best of all, with the exception of two suites, every room has a view of the lake. An indoor pool is another big plus. To find this hotel, take the complimentary airport shuttle or head straight out of the airport, drive under the I-205 overpass, and watch for the hotel sign ahead on the left.

11518 NE Glenn Widing Dr., Portland, OR 97220. ℂ 800/205-7892 or 503/252-2222. Fax 503/257-7008. www.scinns.com. 102 units. $109–$129 double; $119–$149 suite. Rates include continental breakfast. Children 18 and under stay free in parent's room. AE, DC, DISC, MC, V. Free parking. **Amenities:** Indoor pool; exercise room; Jacuzzi; courtesy airport shuttle; business center; guest laundry; dry cleaning. *In room:* A/C, TV, dataport, fridge, coffeemaker, hair dryer, iron, free local calls, high-speed Internet access.

6 Westside Suburbs

INEXPENSIVE

The Lakeshore Inn ℛ *(Finds)* *(Kids)*   Considering that the town of Lake Oswego is Portland's most affluent bedroom community, this motel is quite reasonably priced. It's right on the shore of the lake, and there's a pool on a deck built on the water's edge, making it a great place to stay in summer. Rooms have standard motel furnishings but are large and have kitchenettes. There are also one- and two-bedroom suites. The 7-mile drive into downtown Portland follows the Willamette River and is quite pleasant. There are several restaurants and cafes within walking distance.

210 N. State St., Lake Oswego, OR 97034. ℂ 800/215-6431 or 503/636-9679. Fax 503/636-6959. www.thelakeshoreinn.com. 33 units. $69–$99 double; $89–$139 suite. Rates include continental breakfast. AE, DC, DISC, MC, V. **Amenities:** Outdoor pool; coin-op laundry. *In room:* A/C, TV, dataport, kitchenette, coffeemaker, hair dryer, iron, free local calls, Wi-Fi.

McMenamins Grand Lodge ℛ   Housed in a former Masonic retirement home, this sprawling lodge 30 to 45 minutes west of Portland in the town of Forest Grove is part of a local microbrewery chain and has a decidedly countercultural feel. Although only five of the rooms here have private bathrooms, there are plenty of well-appointed bathrooms, and most rooms do have sinks. There's also lots of colorful artwork incorporated into the design of the building. However, the main attractions here are the brewpub, the beer garden, and numerous small lounges scattered around the main building. The lodge is surrounded by huge lawns and has its own disc golf course, wine bar, and movie theater.

3505 Pacific Ave., Forest Grove, OR 97116. ℂ 877/922-9533 or 503/992-9533. www.thegrandlodge.com. 77 units (5 with private bathroom). $45–$85 double with shared bathroom; $95–$185 double with private bathroom. Rates include full breakfast. Children 6 and under stay free in parent's room. AE, DC, DISC, MC, V. **Amenities:** 2 restaurants (American); 4 lounges; soaking pool; day spa; massage. *In room:* No phone, Wi-Fi.

5

Where to Dine

The Portland restaurant scene is jumping, and the city has developed a reputation to rival Seattle's when it comes to great restaurants. Several distinct dining districts are full of upscale spots, and though you aren't likely to choose to eat at one of these places on the spur of the moment (reservations are usually imperative), their proximity allows you to check out a few places before making a decision later.

The Pearl District's renovated warehouses currently house the trendiest restaurants, while Nob Hill's Northwest 21st Avenue boasts half a dozen terrific establishments within a few blocks. The Sellwood and Westmoreland neighborhoods of southeast Portland make up another of the city's hot restaurant districts, and for good, inexpensive food, it's hard to beat the many offerings along Northeast Broadway in the Irvington neighborhood, and along North Mississippi Avenue in north Portland.

Dinner in Portland isn't complete without an Oregon wine. Pinot noir and pinot gris, in particular, receive widespread acclaim. However, they can be more expensive than other domestic wines.

1 Downtown (Including the Skidmore Historic District & Chinatown)

EXPENSIVE

The Heathman Restaurant and Bar ✦✦✦ NORTHWEST/ FRENCH This grande dame of Northwest-style restaurants serves Northwest cuisine with a French accent. James Beard-award-winning chef Philippe Boulot changes his menu seasonally, but one thing remains constant: The ingredients used are the very freshest of Oregon and Northwest seafood, meat, wild game, and produce. The interior is Art Deco inspired, the atmosphere bistrolike. An extensive wine list spotlights Oregon wines. The Heathman Hotel has an extensive collection of classic and contemporary art, and on the restaurant walls you'll find Andy Warhol's *Endangered Species* series.

In the Heathman Hotel, 1001 SW Broadway. ✆ 503/790-7752. Reservations highly recommended. Main courses $8.50–$18 lunch, $17–$30 dinner. AE, DC,

Where to Dine in Portland

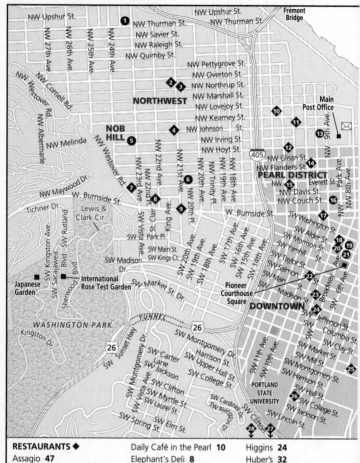

RESTAURANTS ◆

Assagio **47**
Baan-Thai Restaurant **26**
Bijou Café **33**
bluehour **15**
Caffe Mingo **4**
Caprial's Bistro & Wine **48**
Carafe Bistro **25**
Castagna **44**
Chart House **27**

Daily Café in the Pearl **10**
Elephant's Deli **8**
Esparza's Tex-Mex Café **38**
Fong Chong **35**
Fratelli **12**
Genoa **42**
Good Dog/Bad Dog **20**
Gotham Building Tavern **36**
The Heathman
    Restaurant **23**

Higgins **24**
Huber's **32**
Jake's Famous Crawfish **17**
Ken's Place **43**
McCormick & Schmick's
    Harborside Restaurant **29**
Newport Bay Restaurant **30**
Nicholas's **39**
patanegra **1**
Paley's Place **3**

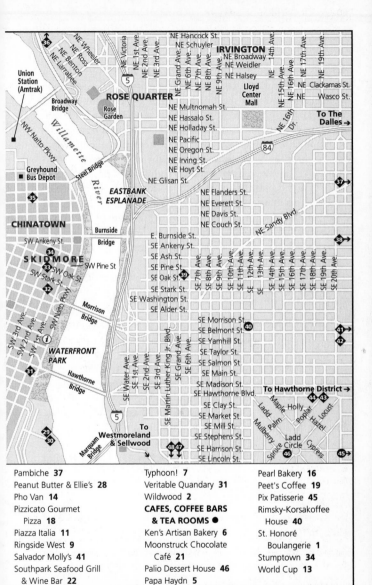

Pambiche **37**	Typhoon! **7**	Pearl Bakery **16**
Peanut Butter & Ellie's **28**	Veritable Quandary **31**	Peet's Coffee **19**
Pho Van **14**	Wildwood **2**	Pix Patisserie **45**
Pizzicato Gourmet	**CAFES, COFFEE BARS**	Rimsky-Korsakoffee
Pizza **18**	**& TEA ROOMS ●**	House **40**
Piazza Italia **11**	Ken's Artisan Bakery **6**	St. Honoré
Ringside West **9**	Moonstruck Chocolate	Boulangerie **1**
Salvador Molly's **41**	Café **21**	Stumptown **34**
Southpark Seafood Grill	Palio Dessert House **46**	World Cup **13**
& Wine Bar **22**	Papa Haydn **5**	

DISC, MC, V. Mon–Thurs 6:30–11am, 11:30am–2pm, and 5–10pm; Fri 6:30–11am, 11:30am–2pm, and 5–11pm; Sat 7am–2pm and 5–11pm; Sun 7am–2pm.

Higgins 🐵🐵🐵 NORTHWEST/MEDITERRANEAN   Higgins strikes a perfect balance between contemporary and classic in both decor and cuisine. The menu, which changes frequently, explores contemporary culinary horizons, while the decor in the tri-level dining room opts for wood paneling and elegant place settings. Yet despite all this, the restaurant remains unpretentious, and portions can be surprisingly generous for a high-end restaurant. Flavors change with the season but are often both subtle and earthy. The honey and chili-glazed pork loin, which comes with seasonal side dishes such as rosemary-roasted potatoes, highlights the restaurant's ability to balance creativity with familiarity. Be sure to leave room for dessert, and if you happen to be a beer lover, you'll be glad to know that Higgins has one of the most interesting beer selections in town (and plenty of good wine, too).

1239 SW Broadway. 🕐 **503/222-9070.** Reservations recommended. Main courses $8–$16 lunch, $19–$30 dinner. AE, DC, MC, V. Mon–Fri 11:30am–2pm and 5–10:30pm; Sat–Sun 5–10:30pm; bistro menu served in the bar daily until midnight.

Veritable Quandary 🐵🐵 NEW AMERICAN   Located in an old brick building just a block off Tom McCall Waterfront Park, this restaurant is a must for summer meals. The restaurant's garden patio, the prettiest in town, faces a small park. The menu changes daily, but keep an eye out for the grilled prawns, and don't pass up the *osso buco.* The chef here pulls in all kinds of influences, so don't be surprised if you find bacon-wrapped dates stuffed with goat cheese or springs rolls filled with duck confit, shiitakes, and Chinese cabbage (served with a side of wasabi-ginger sauce).

1220 SW 1st Ave. 🕐 **503/227-7342.** www.veritablequandary.com. Reservations recommended. Main courses $12–$15 lunch, $16–$29 dinner. AE, DC, DISC, MC, V. Mon–Fri 11:30am–3pm and 5–10pm; Sat–Sun 9:30am–3pm and 5–10pm.

MODERATE

There's an outpost of **Typhoon!** at 400 SW Broadway (🕐 **503/224-8285**), in the Hotel Lucía. See the complete review on p. 46.

Carafe Bistro 🐵🐵 FRENCH   With its small zinc bar, wicker patio chairs, and warm interior hues, Carafe feels just the way you'd expect a neighborhood bistro in Paris to feel. The menu is simple bistro fare (everything from baked escargot to *croque monsieur*), and there are economical nightly three-course prix fixe dinners for $20. With many appetizers, salads, and side dishes, you can easily assemble a thoroughly

Gallic meal. On top of all this, Carafe is right across the street from Keller Auditorium.

200 SW Market St. ℭ **503/248-0004**. Main courses $7.50–$13 lunch, $14–$20 dinner. AE, DC, DISC, MC, V. Mon–Thurs 11am–9pm; Fri 11am–10pm; Sat 5–10pm.

Huber's ℛ *Finds* AMERICAN   Huber's, Portland's oldest restaurant, first opened its doors to the public in 1879 and is tucked inside the Oregon Pioneer Building down a quiet hallway. The main room has a vaulted stained-glass ceiling, Philippine mahogany paneling, and the original brass cash register. Turkey dinner with all the trimmings is the house specialty, but you can also gobble stir-fried turkey and prawns, turkey potpie, and even turkey picatta. Another specialty is Spanish coffee made with rum, Kahlúa, Triple Sec, coffee, and cream. The preparation, which involves flaming the rum in a wineglass, is a very impressive tableside production. Because Huber's bar is quite popular, you'll probably enjoy your meal more if you come for lunch instead of dinner. Be sure to ask for a table in the old vaulted room.

411 SW 3rd Ave. ℭ **503/228-5686**. www.hubers.com. Reservations recommended. Main courses $7–$25. AE, DC, DISC, MC, V. Mon–Thurs 11:30am–4pm and 5–10pm; Fri 11:30am–4pm and 5–11pm; Sat noon–4pm and 5–11pm.

Jake's Famous Crawfish ℛℛ SEAFOOD   Jake's has been a Portland institution since 1909, and the back bar came all the way around Cape Horn in 1880. Much of the rest of the decor looks just as old and well worn as the bar, and therein lies this restaurant's charm. However, it's the great seafood at reasonable prices that makes this place a real winner. There's a daily menu listing a dozen or more specials, but there's really no question about what to eat at Jake's: crawfish, which are always on the menu and served several different ways. Monday through Friday from 3 to 6pm, bar appetizers are only $1.95. The noise level after work, when local businesspeople pack the bar, can be high, and the wait for a table can be long if you don't make a reservation. However, don't let these obstacles put you off.

401 SW 12th Ave. ℭ **503/226-1419**. www.jakesfamouscrawfish.com. Reservations recommended. Main courses $6–$15 lunch, $12–$32 dinner. AE, DC, DISC, MC, V. Mon–Thurs 11am–11pm; Fri–Sat 11am–midnight; Sun 3–11pm.

McCormick and Schmick's Harborside at the Marina ℛℛ SEAFOOD   Anchoring the opposite end of RiverPlace Esplanade from the RiverPlace hotel, this large glitzy seafood restaurant serves up a view of the Willamette and excellent seafood. Four dining levels ensure everyone a view of the river and marina below, and in summer, customers head out to tables on the sidewalk. Because it's so popular, the place tends to be noisy, and the help can sometimes be a bit harried; however, this doesn't detract from the fine food. Although seafood (such as tombo tuna with port wine and cranberries, or salmon and halibut sautéed with forest mushrooms, hazelnuts, and berries) is the main attraction here, the menu is quite extensive. The clientele is mostly upscale, especially at lunch and during the after-work hours.

0309 SW Montgomery St. ✆ **503/220-1865.** www.mccormickandschmicks.com. Reservations recommended. Main courses $12–$27. AE, DC, DISC, MC, V. Sun–Thurs 11am–10pm; Fri–Sat 11am–11pm.

Newport Bay Restaurant ✿ *(Kids)* SEAFOOD   Though there are Newport Bay restaurants all over the Portland area, this one has by far the best location—floating on the Willamette River. Located in the marina at Portland's RiverPlace shopping-and-dining complex, the Newport Bay provides excellent views of the river and the city skyline, especially from the deck. Popular with young couples, families, and boaters, this place exudes a cheery atmosphere, and service is efficient. Nearly everything on the menu has some sort of seafood in it, even the sandwiches, salads, and pastas. Entrees are straightforward and well prepared—nothing too fancy. Sunday brunch is a very good deal.

0425 SW Montgomery St. ✆ **503/227-3474.** www.newportbay.com. Reservations recommended. Main courses $8–$22. AE, DC, DISC, MC, V. Mon–Thurs 11am–11pm; Fri–Sat 11am–midnight; Sun 10am–11pm. Closes 1 hr. earlier Oct–May.

Southpark Seafood Grill & Wine Bar ✿✿ *(Value)* MEDITERRANEAN/SEAFOOD   With its high ceiling; long, heavy drapes; and interesting wall mural, the wine bar here is a contemporary interpretation of late-19th-century Paris, and the main dining room is both comfortable and classy. For a starter, don't pass up the fried calamari, rock shrimp, and vegetables served with spicy aioli. Equally delicious: the butternut squash and ricotta-filled ravioli with toasted hazelnuts, which comes in a rich Marsala wine sauce that begs to be sopped up with the crusty bread. An extensive wine list presents some compelling choices, and the desserts are consistently excellent.

901 SW Salmon St. ✆ **503/326-1300.** www.southpark.citysearch.com. Reservations recommended. Main courses $8.50–$15 lunch, $14–$24 dinner. AE, MC, V. Mon–Thurs 11:30am–3pm and 5–10pm; Fri 11:30am–3pm and 5–11pm; Sat 11am–3pm and 5–11pm; Sun 11am–3pm and 5–10pm.

INEXPENSIVE
Baan-Thai Restaurant ✿ *(Finds)* THAI   Everyone in Portland seems to have a favorite Thai restaurant, and, while Baan-Thai may

not show up on local "Best of Portland" lists, it should. It's cheap, it's casual, and it's pretty conveniently located. However, best of all, this place does awesome fish dishes. Try the Niagara fish (a whole fried fish topped with spicy lime sauce) or the Panang salmon in creamy curry sauce. The volcano chicken, which is actually a whole game hen baked and then fried and served with Thai barbecue sauce, is another must-have.

1924 SW Broadway. ℭ 503/224-8424. Main courses $6–$15. MC, V. Mon–Sat 11am–10pm.

Bijou Café ℛ NATURAL FOODS　The folks who run the Bijou take both food and health seriously. They'll serve you a bowl of steamed brown rice and raisins for breakfast, but you can also get delicious fresh oyster hash or brioche French toast. However, the real hits here are the sautéed potatoes and the muffins, which come with full breakfasts. Don't leave without trying them. Local and organic products are used as often as possible at this comfortably old-fashioned yet thoroughly modern cafe.

132 SW 3rd Ave. ℭ 503/222-3187. Breakfast and lunch $6.50–$13. MC, V. Mon–Fri 7am–2pm; Sat–Sun 8am–2pm.

Fong Chong ℛ CHINESE　This place may not look like much from the outside (or from the inside, for that matter), but the throngs of people crowding the tables in the middle of the day should give you an idea that this place does good dim sum. This traditional Chinese midday meal of small plates is ordered off carts that are wheeled around the dining room and is served daily between 10:30am and 3pm. With lots of steamed dumplings, pot stickers, and shrimp balls, it's easy to order more than you can eat. Pace yourself. Located 2 blocks from the Portland Classical Chinese Garden, this is a great place to stick with the Chinese theme after a visit to the gardens.

301 NW 4th Ave. ℭ 503/228-6868. Main courses $6–$12; dim sum $3–$6. MC, V. Daily 10:30am–10pm.

2 Northwest Portland (Including the Pearl District & Nob Hill)

EXPENSIVE

Bluehour ℛ FRENCH/ITALIAN　Restaurateur Bruce Carey has long dominated the Portland restaurant scene, and at this high-style restaurant, he continues to woo and wow the local trendsetters. Located in a converted warehouse that serves as headquarters for Portland advertising giant Wieden+Kennedy, Bluehour has a very theatrical atmosphere. With sophisticated menu items such as seared foie gras and American sturgeon caviar, and superb service, it's obvious that Bluehour is Portland's most haute restaurant. However, this is also the sort of place where being seen by the right people is as important as the food.

250 NW 13th Ave. © 503/226-3394. www.bluehouronline.com. Reservations highly recommended. Main dishes $20–$49. AE, DISC, MC, V. Tues–Thurs 5:30–10pm; Fri–Sat 5:30–10:30pm.

Paley's Place ☆☆ NORTHWEST/FRENCH   Located in a Victorian-era house, Paley's is a favorite of Portland foodies. Chef Vitaly Paley continues to receive accolades year after year and in 2005 won a James Beard award. The menu relies extensively on the freshest local organic ingredients (often stacked in baskets on the front porch) and ranges from traditional bistro fare to dishes with complex flavors and a hint of Northwest inspiration. Whether you're in the mood for spit-roasted suckling pit or corn-and-crab risotto, you'll certainly find something appealing. If you've never tried sweetbreads, this is the place to do so, and the signature *frites,* with a mustard aioli, are not to be missed. Big on wines, Paley's offers wine tasting on Wednesdays. For dessert, I can't pass up the warm chocolate soufflé with outrageously rich house-made ice cream. Inside, the restaurant is small and stylishly comfortable but can be quite noisy.

1204 NW 21st Ave. © **503/243-2403.** www.paleysplace.citysearch.com. Reservations highly recommended. Main courses $21–$35. AE, MC, V. Mon–Thurs 5:30–10pm; Fri–Sat 5:30–11pm; Sun 5–10pm.

RingSide Downtown ☆ STEAK   Despite the location on a rather unattractive stretch of West Burnside Street, RingSide has long been a favorite Portland steakhouse. Boxing may be the main theme of the restaurant, but the name is a two-fisted pun that also refers to the incomparable onion rings that are an essential part of any meal here. Have your rings with a side order of one of their perfectly cooked steaks for a real knockout meal. The three-course prix fixe dinners are only $25 if you order before 5:45pm or after 9pm.

2165 W. Burnside St. © **503/223-1513.** www.ringsidesteakhouse.com. Reservations highly recommended. Steaks $26–$38; other main courses $18–$47; prix fixe dinner $25–$35. AE, DISC, MC, V. Mon–Sat 5pm–midnight; Sun 4–11:30pm.

Wildwood ☆☆ NEW AMERICAN   With a menu that changes daily and a spare, elegant interior decor straight out of *Architectural Digest,* Wildwood has for many years been one of Portland's best restaurants. If you love creative cuisine, be sure to give this place a try. Fresh seasonal ingredients combined into simple yet imaginative dishes are the hallmark of chef Cory Schreiber's cooking, and often there are no more than a handful of ingredients in a dish, so as to let each of the flavors shine through. On a recent evening, there were skillet-roasted Washington mussels with garlic, sun-dried tomato, and saffron, and an excellent oyster-topped salad with bacon and aioli. This is the only non-Indian restaurant I know of that has a tandoor oven, and you can usually count on the meat dishes that are roasted in this oven. Salads and sorbets are exceptionally good. If you can't get a reservation, you can usually get served in the bar.

1221 NW 21st Ave. (503/248-9663. www.wildwoodrestaurant.com. Reservations highly recommended. Main courses $12–$14 lunch, $18–$37 dinner. AE, MC, V. Mon–Thurs 11:30am–2:30pm and 5:30–9pm; Fri–Sat 11:30am–2:30pm and 5:30–10pm; Sun 5–8:30pm.

MODERATE

Caffe Mingo 👯👯 *Finds* ITALIAN   This intimate little neighborhood restaurant has terrific food, an interior as attractive as that of any other upscale restaurant here on northwest Portland's restaurant row, and lower prices. If there's any problem with this immensely popular place, it's that you almost always have to wait for a table and they only take reservations for larger parties. The solution? Get here as early as possible. The menu is short and focuses on painstakingly prepared Italian comfort food. Just about all of the items on the menu are winners, from the antipasto platter, which might include roasted fennel, fresh mozzarella, and roasted red pepper, to an unusual penne pasta dish with tender beef braised in chianti and espresso. The *panna cotta* dessert ("cooked cream" with fruit) is reason enough to come back here again and again, even if you have to wait in the rain to get a seat.

807 NW 21st Ave. (503/226-4646. Reservations accepted only for parties of 6 or more. Main courses $10–$20. AE, DC, DISC, MC, V. Sun–Thurs 5–10pm; Fri–Sat 5–10:30pm.

Fratelli 👯👯 REGIONAL ITALIAN   In this rustic-yet-chic restaurant, cement walls provide a striking contrast to dramatic draperies and candles that drip casually onto the tabletops. Dishes are consistently good, with surprisingly moderate prices for the Pearl District. There's excellent olive oil to go with your bread and an antipasto plate that might include spring beans with arugula and octopus, chicken wrapped in prosciutto, rabbit *crepinette* (a sort of sausage), or a luscious savory panna cotta. The polenta with wild mushrooms and the seared chicken wrapped in prosciutto are long-time favorites here. This restaurant's aesthetic and menu are similar to Caffe Mingo's (see above), but at Fratelli you can make reservations.

1230 NW Hoyt St. ⟡ **503/241-8800.** Reservations recommended. Main courses $13–$20. AE, DC, MC, V. Sun–Thurs 4:30–9:30pm; Fri–Sat 4:30–10:30pm.

patanegra ⟡⟡ *Finds* SPANISH   Located next door to one of my favorite bakeries, this Spanish restaurant is the reincarnation of one of Portland's first tapas places. Tapas (Spanish small plates) are still the mainstays of the menu here, but patanegra also serves a few different types of paella. Still, I can't ever get past all the flavor-packed little tapas plates. The best way to approach this rather exotic menu is to just start ordering whatever sounds most interesting and then order more if your first round doesn't fill you up. Let me warn you, though, that the tapas menu is heavy on proteins and starches, and a bit light on veggies. Oh well, you can always have a salad tomorrow.

1818 NW 23rd Place. ⟡ **503/227-7282.** www.patanegra-restaurant.com. Main courses $19; tapas $6–$10. AE, MC, V. Tues–Fri 11:30am–11pm; Sat 5–11pm.

Pho Van ⟡⟡ VIETNAMESE   If you think of Formica tables and fluorescent lights when you think of Vietnamese restaurants, think again. This is one of the most stylish restaurants in town, with decor drawing on a modern Asian aesthetic. The prices, however, are extremely reasonable. As the name implies, you can get flavorful *pho* soup (a Vietnamese staple), but I prefer the dishes from the grill and the other more substantial entrees, as well as the crispy crepes filled with shrimp, scallops, and vegetables.

1012 NW Glisan St. ⟡ **503/248-2172.** Reservations recommended. Main courses $8–$15 lunch, $8.50–$19 dinner. AE, DISC, MC, V. Mon–Sat 11am–3pm and 5–10pm.

Piazza Italia ⟡⟡ ITALIAN   Portland has more than its fair share of good Italian restaurants, but none feels as much like a trip to Italy as this one. The staff speaks Italian most of the time, and the TV over the bar is tuned to Italian soap operas and soccer matches. Just inside the front door is a glass case full of the imported meats, cheeses, and olives that go into the antipasto plate. This place is small and has a very limited menu, but it's always bustling. Try the simple linguine *squarciarella,* which is made with eggs, prosciutto, onions, and Parmesan cheese. During the summer, the tables on the sidewalk are the in-demand seats.

1129 NW Johnson St. ⟡ **503/478-0619.** www.piazzaportland.com. Main courses $9.50–$14. AE, DISC, MC, V. Mon–Sat noon–10pm; Sun noon–8pm.

Typhoon! ☞ THAI Located just off Northwest 23rd Avenue, this trendy spot is a bit pricey for a Thai restaurant, but the unusual menu offerings generally aren't available at other Portland Thai restaurants. Be sure to start a meal with the *miang kum,* which consists of dried shrimp, tiny chilies, ginger, lime, peanuts, shallots, and toasted coconut drizzled with a sweet-and-sour sauce and wrapped up in a spinach leaf. The burst of flavors on your taste buds is absolutely astounding. (I first had this in Thailand and waited years to get it in the United States.) The whole front wall of the restaurant slides away for Thai-style open-air dining in the summer. There is an extensive tea list.

There's another **Typhoon!** at 410 SW Broadway (✆ **503/224-8285**), in the Hotel Lućia.

2310 NW Everett St. ✆ **503/243-7557.** www.typhoonrestaurants.com. Reservations recommended. Main courses $9–$18. AE, DC, DISC, MC, V. Mon–Thurs 11:30am–2pm and 4:30–9pm; Fri 11:30am–2pm and 4:30–10pm; Sat noon–3pm and 4:30–10pm; Sun noon–3pm and 4:30–9pm.

INEXPENSIVE

Daily Café in the Pearl ☞ AMERICAN/SANDWICHES Healthful, flavorful breakfasts and creative sandwiches are the mainstays of this hip-yet-casual urban cafe in the heart of the Pearl District. On sunny days, take your meal out onto the converted loading dock and ogle all the buff people coming and going from the area's gym, personal trainer, and workout-clothing store. Although grilled vegetarian panini and wasabi tuna salad may better sum up the culinary aesthetics here, they also do a mean bacon cheeseburger. This is primarily a lunch spot, but dinners are also served.

902 NW 13th Ave. ✆ **503/242-1916.** Main courses $4–$6.50. MC, V. Mon–Tues 7am–5pm; Wed–Sat 7am–9:30pm; Sun 9am–2pm.

Elephant's Deli ☞ DELI This is definitely not your corner deli. This is a deli with a capital *D,* and it pushes the boundaries of what can even be considered a deli. Elephant's is a behemoth of a deli, which, of course, makes the name appropriate, and it's mouthwateringly diverse in its food offerings. Whether you want some pastrami to go or a full gourmet meal, you can get it here, which makes this the best place in town to put together a picnic before heading up to Washington Park. Want a cocktail? They've got a full bar here, and plenty of good appetizers to accompany the drinks. Now, don't you wish you had one of these pachyderms in your town?

115 NW 22nd Ave. ✆ **503/299-6304.** www.elephantsdeli.com. Reservations not accepted. Main courses $5–$15. AE, MC, V. Mon–Sat 7am–8:30pm; Sun 9:30am–6:30pm.

3 Southwest Portland

EXPENSIVE

Chart House 👭👭 SEAFOOD   Although this place is a part of a restaurant chain with lots of outposts all over the country, it also happens to boast the best view of any restaurant in Portland. On top of that, it serves the best New England clam chowder in the state. While you savor your chowder, you can marvel at the views of the Willamette River, Mount Hood, Mount St. Helens, and nearly all of Portland's east side. Fresh fish—either grilled, baked, or blackened—is the house specialty. You'll also find a selection of excellent steaks for the problem diner in your group who just won't eat seafood. No dinner here is complete without the hot chocolate lava cake, which has to be ordered at the start of your meal if you want it to be ready when you are. I recommend coming here for lunch or the early-bird dinner specials, which cost $15 to $17 and are available Sunday through Thursday between 5 and 6:30pm.

The Chart House is in an out-of-the-way spot about a 10-minute drive from downtown Portland; be sure to call ahead and get driving directions.

5700 SW Terwilliger Blvd. ℂ 503/246-6963. www.chart-house.com. Reservations recommended. Main courses $8–$25 lunch, $17–$40 dinner. AE, DC, DISC, MC, V. Mon–Fri 11:30am–2:30pm and 5–10pm; Sat–Sun 5–10pm.

INEXPENSIVE

Peanut Butter & Ellie's 👭 *(Finds)* *(Kids)* AMERICAN   This cozy, colorful spot in an upscale southwest Portland neighborhood takes kid-friendly to the extreme. This place is exclusively for children, though their parents are welcome if they are well-behaved. The menu features—you guessed it—peanut-butter-and-jelly sandwiches (some topped with grapes, raisins, or even shredded carrots). Okay, so there are soups, salads, chicken sandwiches and grilled cheese sandwiches, and a few other offerings, but the peanut butter constructions are the real highlights. Most of the tables are kid-size, but there are a few for adults. Oh, and by the way, the peanut butter is organic and is ground right here.

4405 SW Vermont St. ℂ 503/282-1783. www.peanutbutterellies.com. Main courses $4.50–$8.50. MC, V. Daily 9am–8pm.

4 North & Northeast Portland

EXPENSIVE

Gotham Building Tavern 𝒢𝒢 NEW AMERICAN/ITALIAN
You won't meet Batman here, and this is definitely no tavern. So you can forget about swilling Pabst Blue Ribbon here. This is one of Portland's best new restaurants and has crafted a thoroughly modern menu and dining space. The walls are stacked with big slabs of woods that lend the dining room a hint of log-cabin chic, and count yourself lucky if you get a table in the section of the dining room that looks like a giant wooden basket. The menu takes simple ingredients and crafts them into memorable dishes such as a dish of porchetta and white beans that was as good as any porchetta I had on my last trip to Italy. Even a simple dish such as bavette pasta with cheese and black pepper can be absolutely delicious in its simplicity. The owners of this restaurant also operate a clarklewis, 1001 SE Water St., and a special reservation-only family-style dining room that is in the same building as the Gotham Building Tavern.

2240 N. Interstate Ave. ℂ **503/235-2294.** www.ripepdx.com. Reservations recommended. Main courses $17–$21. AE, MC, V. Tues–Thurs 8am–2:30pm and 5–9pm; Fri 8am–2:30pm and 5–10pm; Sat 9am–2pm and 5–10pm; Sun 9am–2pm and 5–9pm.

MODERATE

Pambiche 𝒢 *Finds* CUBAN   Driving past this tiny hole-in-the-wall neighborhood eatery, you'd never guess that it's one of Portland's most popular restaurants. However, you can't pass the tropical

---

Kids Family-Friendly Restaurants

Bijou Café (p. 63)   Parents who care about the food their children eat will want to bring the family to this cozy old-fashioned diner that serves great breakfasts made with organic ingredients.

Newport Bay Restaurant (p. 62)   A cheery atmosphere, straightforward meals, and a great location on the Willamette River make this a good family pick.

Peanut Butter & Ellie's (p. 68)   This place isn't just family friendly; it's designed exclusively for kids—and, of course, the various peanut-butter-and-jelly sandwiches are big hits with the little ones.

hot pink building without giving it a glance. Don't just gawk—get in there! The food is straight out of Havana, with taro-root fritters, codfish-and-potato croquettes, fried yucca root, and fried bananas. And that's just on the appetizer list. Just don't fill up on all those tasty little tropical treats; the main dishes, such as shrimp Creole, Cuban-style beef hash, and oxtail braised in red wine, are all served in huge portions.

2811 NE Glisan St. ⓒ 503/233-0511. Main courses $6.50–$10 lunch, $8–$18 dinner. MC, V. Sun–Thurs 11am–10pm; Fri–Sat 11am–midnight.

5 Southeast Portland

VERY EXPENSIVE

Genoa 🐦🐦🐦 REGIONAL ITALIAN   This has long been the best Italian restaurant in Portland, and with fewer than a dozen tables, it's also one of the smallest. Everything, from the breads to the luscious desserts, is made fresh in the kitchen with the best local seasonal ingredients. This is an ideal setting for a romantic dinner, and service is attentive—the waiter explains dishes in detail as they are served, and dishes are magically whisked away as they're finished. The fixed-price menu changes every 3 weeks, but a typical dinner might start with a little pork-stuffed crepe topped with warm apple-quince sauce and onion marmalade. Follow that with butternut squash soup, wild-mushroom pasta, and a pear salad before arriving at the main course, which might be something like medallions of monkfish in a red-wine reduction sauce or duck breast with a port-wine-and-peppercorn sauce. It takes Herculean restraint to choose among chocolate and nut tortes, fresh berry tarts, or liqueur-infused desserts.

2832 SE Belmont St. ⓒ 503/238-1464. www.genoarestaurant.com. Reservations required. Fixed-price 4-course dinner $60; 7-course dinner $75. AE, DC, DISC, MC, V. Daily 5:30–9:30pm (4-course dinner limited to 5:30 and 6pm seatings only).

EXPENSIVE

Caprial's Bistro and Wine 🐦🐦 NORTHWEST   If you're a foodie, you're probably already familiar with celebrity chef Caprial Pence, who helped put the Northwest on the national restaurant map and has since gone on to write several cookbooks and host TV and radio food shows. That her eponymously named restaurant is a fairly casual place tucked away in a quiet residential neighborhood in Southeast Portland may come as a surprise. The menu changes monthly and is limited to four or five main dishes and about twice as many appetizers. Entrees combine perfectly cooked meat and seasonal seafood dishes with vibrant sauces. Desserts are usually rich without being overly sweet. There is also a wine bar offering a superb selection of wines at reasonable prices.

7015 SE Milwaukie Ave. (*© 503/236-6457*. www.caprial.com. Reservations highly recommended. Main courses $7.75–$12 lunch, $18–$28 dinner. AE, MC, V. Tues–Thurs 11:30am–2:30pm and 5–9pm; Fri–Sat 11:30am–2:30pm and 5–9:30pm.

Castagna ✸✸ FRENCH/ITALIAN Located on a rather non-descript stretch of Hawthorne Boulevard and much removed from the bustle of this boulevard's central commercial area, Castagna is a magnet for Portland foodies. Considering the less than stylish location and minimalist (though thoroughly designed) interior, it's obvious that the food's the thing here. Dishes tend toward simple preparations that allow the freshness of the ingredients to express themselves. Entrees such as black cod with parsnip-sunchoke purée, porcini mushrooms, and pea shoots, sum up the dominant culinary aesthetic at this restaurant. In addition to the main dining room, there is an inexpensive cafe serving much simpler fare.

1752 SE Hawthorne Blvd. (*© **503/231-7373**. www.castagnarestaurant.com. Reservations highly recommended. Main dishes $18–$28; cafe main courses $11–$19. AE, DISC, MC, V. Main restaurant Wed–Thurs 5:30–9:30pm, Fri–Sat 5:30–10:30pm; cafe Mon–Thurs 5:30–10pm, Fri–Sat 5:30–11pm, Sun 5–9:30pm.

MODERATE

Assaggio ✸✸ RUSTIC ITALIAN This trattoria in the Sellwood neighborhood focuses on pastas and wines; the menu lists lots of pastas, and the wine list includes dozens of Italian wines, some of which are rarely encountered in the U.S. The atmosphere in this tiny place is theatrical, with indirect lighting, dark walls, and the likes of Mario Lanza playing in the background. Don't be surprised if after taking your first bite you suddenly hear a Verdi aria. The pastas, with surprisingly robust flavors, are the main attraction. *Assaggio* means a sampling or a taste, and that is exactly what you get if you order pasta Assaggio style—a sampling of several dishes, all served family style. This is especially fun if you're here with a group.

7742 SE 13th Ave. (*© **503/232-6151**. www.assaggiorestaurant.com. Reservations recommended. Main courses $11–$19. AE, MC, V. Mon–Thurs 11am–2:30pm and 5–9:30pm; Fri–Sat 11am–2:30pm and 5–10pm; Sun 5–9:30pm.

Ken's Place ✸ *Value* AMERICAN REGIONAL It's just a tiny retro diner with framed crocheted potholders on the walls, but chef/owner Ken Gordon turns out dishes here that would do justice to the best restaurants in town. On any given night, there might be only half a dozen entrees, but these economically priced dishes might include chianti-braised pork leg with raisins and olives, or an Asian-style pork chop with ginger applesauce. There are always plenty of side dishes with which to fill out a meal. Desserts such as chewy caramel pecan tart should not be missed. This casual neighborhood place is the absolute antithesis of Portland's chic restaurants, but the food is every bit as good. Desserts are stacked on a desk just inside the front door, so you'll know what you're saving room for.

1852 SE Hawthorne Blvd. ℂ **503/236-9520.** Reservations not accepted. Main courses $9.25–$20. MC, V. Tues–Sat 5:30–9:30pm.

INEXPENSIVE

Esparza's Tex-Mex Café ⊛ *(Kids)* TEX-MEX   With red-eyed cow skulls on the walls and marionettes, model planes, and stuffed iguanas and armadillos hanging from the ceiling, the decor here can be described only as Tex-eclectic, a description that is just as appropriately applied to the menu. Sure, there are enchiladas and tamales and tacos, but they might be filled with ostrich or buffalo. Rest assured, Esparza's also serves standard ingredients such as chicken and beef. Main courses come with some pretty good rice and beans, and if you want your meal hotter, they'll toss you a couple of jalapeño peppers. The *nopalitos* (fried cactus) are worth a try, and the margaritas are some of the best in Portland. While you're waiting for a seat (there's almost always a wait), check out the vintage tunes on the jukebox.

2725 SE Ankeny St. ℂ **503/234-7909.** Reservations not accepted. Main courses $8.50–$18. AE, DC, DISC, MC, V. Mon–Sat 11:30am–10pm (in summer Fri–Sat until 10:30pm).

Nicholas's *(Finds)* MIDDLE EASTERN   This little hole in the wall on an unattractive stretch of Grand Avenue is usually packed at mealtimes, and it's not the decor or ambience that pulls people in. The big draw is the great food and cheap prices. In spite of the heat from the pizza oven and the crowded conditions, the customers and waitstaff still manage to be friendly. Our favorite dish is the *Manakish,* Mediterranean pizza with thyme, oregano, sesame seeds, olive oil, and lemony-flavored sumac. Also available are a creamy hummus, baba ghanouj, kabobs, falafel, and gyros.

318 SE Grand Ave. (between Pine and Oak sts.). ℂ **503/235-5123.** www.nicholas-restaurant.com. Reservations not accepted. Main courses $4.75–$11. No credit cards. Mon–Sat 11am–9pm; Sun noon–9pm.

Salvador Molly's ⚸ (Finds) CARIBBEAN   With lots of colorful mismatched tables and chairs and a funky, tropical decor, this Caribbean restaurant is a real hot spot. Flavors are in your face, servings are big, and prices are low. Best of all, this self-styled pirate cookin' is a surefire antidote to a gray winter day. What's not to love? With lots of spicy starters, this is also a great spot for a light meal. Be forewarned, however, that the food here can be fiery. There's even a "Wall of Flame" for people who can survive Salvador Molly's great balls of fire—habanero-spiked cheese fritters. For tamer tastes, try the *arepas* (Venezuelan corn cakes), the oyster taco, or tamales steamed in banana leaves.

3350 SE Morrison St. (✆) 503/234-0896. www.salvadormollys.com. Main courses $8.25–$14. AE, DISC, MC, V. Mon–Thurs 4:30–10pm; Fri 4:30pm–midnight; Sat noon–midnight; Sun noon–10pm.

6 Coffee, Tea, Bakeries & Pastry Shops

CAFES

If you'd like to sample some cafes around Portland that not only serve the full range of coffee drinks but also are atmospheric, I recommend the following:

With an upscale Starbucks-style interior decor, a social conscience, and a Pearl District location, **World Cup,** 721 NW Ninth Ave. (✆ 503/546-7377), is a coffee haven for the politically correct. It's even located in an unusual environmentally friendly "green" building that has a rooftop terrace. Other World Cups are located inside Powell's City of Books, 1005 W. Burnside St. (✆ 503/228-4651, ext. 234), and in the Nob Hill neighborhood at 1740 NW Glisan St. (✆ 503/228-4152).

There's many a Portlander who swears by the coffee at **Stumptown Coffee Roasters,** 128 SW Third Ave. (✆ 503/295-6144), a big, trendy cafe with an art-school aesthetic. Whether you go for the French press or a double shot of espresso, you're sure to be satisfied. Over on the east side of the Willamette River are Stumptown's two original cafes: 3377 SE Division St. (✆ 503/230-7797) and 3356 SE Belmont St. (✆ 503/232-8889), which both tend to attract a young, hip clientele.

If coffee isn't your cup of choice and hot chocolate is, then be sure to stop by **Moonstruck Chocolate Café,** 608 SW Alder St. (✆ 503/241-0955), where you can choose from a wide variety of hot chocolate drinks. There's another Moonstruck in the Nob Hill neighborhood at 526 NW 23rd Ave. (✆ 503/542-3400).

BAKERIES, PASTRY SHOPS & GELATERIAS

Pearl Bakery &&, 102 NW Ninth Ave. (© **503/827-0910**), in the heart of the Pearl District, is famous in Portland for its breads and European-style pastries. The gleaming bakery cafe is also good for sandwiches, such as a roasted eggplant and tomato pesto on crusty bread.

Say the words *Papa Haydn* to a Portlander, and you'll see a blissful smile appear. What is it about this little bistro that sends locals into accolades of superlatives? The desserts. The lemon chiffon torte, raspberry gâteau, black velvet, and tiramisu at **Papa Haydn West** &&, 701 NW 23rd Ave. (© **503/228-7317**), are legendary. There's another location at 5829 SE Milwaukie Ave. (© **503/232-9440**) in Sellwood.

Also in the Nob Hill neighborhood, you'll find **Ken's Artisan Bakery,** 338 NW 21st Ave. (© **503/248-2202;** www.kensartisan.com), which doesn't do a wide variety of pastries. However, what it does do, it does very well. Yum! Try the fruit tarts. However, my current favorite bakery in the neighborhood is the utterly Gallic **St. Honoré Boulangerie,** 2335 NW Thurman St. (© **503/445-4342;** www.sainthonorebakery.com). Not only does this place turn out awesome pastries and breads, but you can read *Le Monde* while eating your croissant.

Located in Ladd's Addition, an old neighborhood full of big trees and craftsman-style bungalows, **Palio Dessert House** &, 1996 SE Ladd Ave. (© **503/232-9412**), is a very relaxed place with a timeless European quality. To get there, take Hawthorne Boulevard east to the corner of 12th and Hawthorne, then go diagonally down Ladd Avenue.

The **Rimsky-Korsakoffee House** &, 707 SE 12th Ave. (© **503/232-2640**), a classic old-style coffeehouse (complete with mismatched chairs), has been Portland's favorite dessert hangout for more than a decade. Live classical music and great desserts keep patrons loyal. (The mocha fudge cake is small but deadly.) Open from 7pm to midnight on Sunday through Thursday, and until 1am on Friday and Saturday.

We've saved the best for last. **Pix Patisserie,** 3402 SE Division St. (© **503/232-4407**), makes by far the most decadent pastries in Portland. Every sweet little jewel here is a work of art, and it can sometimes be a real challenge to desecrate these creations with a fork. Go ahead, take a bite. You won't soon forget the experience!

If it's hot out and nothing will do but something cold and creamy, check out one of Portland's gelaterias. These Italian-style frozen-dessert parlors have taken Portland by storm. In the Nob Hill neighborhood, there's **Alotto Gelato,** 931 NW 23rd Ave. (© **503/ 228-1709**); in the Pearl District, try **Mio Gelato,** 25 NW 11th Ave. (© **503/226-8002**); and over in northeast Portland, just off East Burnside Street, there's **Staccato Gelato,** 232 NE 28th (© **503/ 231-7100**).

7 Quick Bites & Cheap Eats

If you're just looking for something quick, cheap, and good to eat, there are lots of great options around the city. Downtown, at **Good Dog/Bad Dog,** 708 SW Alder St. (© **503/222-3410**), you'll find handmade sausages. The bratwurst with kraut and onions is a good deal.

Designer pizzas topped with anything from roasted eggplant to wild mushrooms to Thai peanut sauce can be had at **Pizzicato Gourmet Pizza** ₭. Find them downtown at 705 SW Alder St. (© **503/226- 1007**); in Northwest Portland at 505 NW 23rd Ave. (© **503/242- 0023**); and in Southeast Portland at 2811 E. Burnside (© **503/ 236-6045**).

6

Exploring Portland

Most American cities boast about their museums and historic buildings, shopping, and restaurants; Portland, as always, is different. Ask a Portlander about the city's must-see attractions, and you'll probably be directed to the Japanese Garden, the International Rose Test Garden, and the Portland Saturday Market.

This isn't to say that the Portland Art Museum, which specializes in blockbuster exhibits, isn't worth visiting or that there are no historic buildings around. It's just that Portland's gardens, thanks to the weather here, are some of the finest in the country. What's more, all the rainy weather seems to keep artists indoors creating beautiful art and crafts for much of the year, work that many artists sell at the Portland Saturday Market.

Gardening is a Portland obsession, and there are numerous world-class public gardens and parks within the city. Visiting all the city's gardens alone can take up 2 or 3 days of touring, so leave plenty of time in your schedule if you have a green thumb.

Once you've seen the big attractions, it's time to start learning why everyone loves living here so much. Portlanders for the most part are active types who enjoy skiing on Mount Hood and hiking in the Columbia Gorge just as much as they enjoy going to art museums, so no visit to Portland would be complete without venturing out into the Oregon countryside. Within 1½ hours you can be skiing on Mount Hood, walking beside the chilly waters of the Pacific, sampling pinot noir in wine country, or hiking beside a waterfall in the Columbia Gorge. However, for those who prefer urban activities, the museums and parks listed below should satisfy.

SUGGESTED ITINERARIES

If You Have 1 Day

Start your day in Washington Park at the **Rose Garden** (the roses are in bloom June–Sept) and the **Japanese Garden** (lovely any time of year). After touring these two gardens, head downhill into downtown Portland. If you can make it to **Pioneer Courthouse**

Square by noon, you can catch the day's weather prediction on the *Weather Machine* sculpture. From here, head over to the South Park Blocks and visit the **Portland Art Museum,** which usually has some big show going on. Across the park from this museum is the **Oregon Historical Society Museum,** where you can finish your day. If it's the weekend, be sure to squeeze in time to visit the **Saturday Market** (open both Sat and Sun; closed Jan–Feb), in the Skidmore Historic District.

If You Have 2 Days

Follow the 1-day strategy as outlined above. On your second day, visit the **Portland Classical Chinese Garden,** explore some of the historic blocks in the **Old Town** neighborhood (take in the Saturday Market if you haven't already), then walk through **Tom McCall Waterfront Park,** which is on the banks of the Willamette River. Take a scenic **cruise** or jet-boat tour on the river or do some quiet paddling on a guided **sea-kayak tour.**

If You Have 3 Days

Follow the outline above for your first 2 days in town. On your third day, head up the **Columbia Gorge** to see its many beautiful waterfalls. If you get an early start, you can loop all the way around **Mount Hood** and maybe get in a little hiking from historic Timberline Lodge.

If You Have 4 Days or More

Follow the 3-day strategy as outlined above. On day 4, head over to the coast; it's only about 1½ hours away. You can stroll around artsy **Cannon Beach** and explore nearby **Ecola State Park.** Then make your way down the coast, stopping at other small state parks along the way. You can head back to Portland from **Tillamook.** If you have time, do part or all of the **Three Capes Scenic Loop** outside of Tillamook before returning to Portland.

On day 5, venture north to **Mount St. Helens** for the day to see the devastation that was caused when this volcano erupted back in 1980. Along the way, you could stop and visit historic Fort Vancouver in **Vancouver, Washington.** If you're a wine fancier, you could also head west from Portland for some **wine tasting.**

1 Downtown Portland's Cultural District

Any visit to Portland should start at the corner of Southwest Broadway and Yamhill Street on **Pioneer Courthouse Square.** The brick-paved square is an outdoor stage for everything from flower displays to concerts to protest rallies, but not too many years ago this beautiful area

Portland Attractions

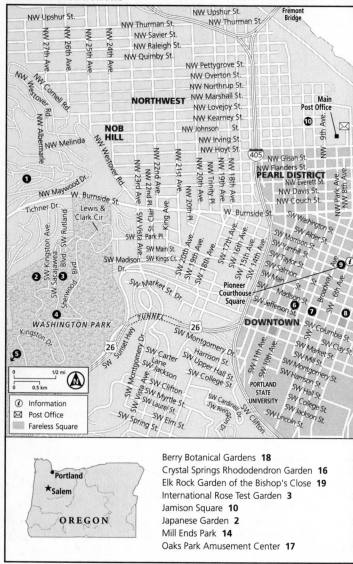

Berry Botanical Gardens **18**
Crystal Springs Rhododendron Garden **16**
Elk Rock Garden of the Bishop's Close **19**
International Rose Test Garden **3**
Jamison Square **10**
Japanese Garden **2**
Mill Ends Park **14**
Oaks Park Amusement Center **17**

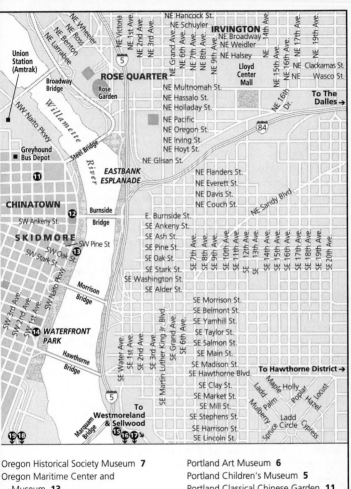

Oregon Historical Society Museum **7**	Portland Art Museum **6**
Oregon Maritime Center and Museum **13**	Portland Children's Museum **5**
	Portland Classical Chinese Garden **11**
Oregon Museum of Science & Industry (OMSI) **15**	*Portlandia* & the Portland Building **8**
Oregon Zoo **5**	Portland Saturday Market **12**
Pioneer Courthouse Square **9**	Washington Park **4**
Pittock Mansion **1**	World Forestry Center Discovery Museum **5**

was nothing but a parking lot. The parking lot had been created in 1951 (in the days before historic preservation) when the Portland Hotel, an architectural gem of a Queen Anne–style château, was torn down.

Today the square, with its tumbling waterfall fountain and free-standing columns, is Portland's favorite gathering spot, especially at noon, when the **Weather Machine** ✸, a mechanical sculpture, forecasts the weather for the next 24 hours. Amid a fanfare of music and flashing lights, the Weather Machine sends up clouds of mist and then either a sun (clear weather), a dragon (stormy weather), or a blue heron (clouds and drizzle) appears.

Keep your eyes on the square's brick pavement, too. Every brick contains a name (or names) or statement, and some are rather curious. Also on the square, you'll find the **Portland Oregon Visitor Association Information Center** and a Starbucks. Unfortunately, you'll also find plenty of street kids hanging out here all hours of the day and night, so don't be surprised if they ask you for spare change.

Also not to be missed in this neighborhood are *Portlandia* ✸✸ and the **Portland Building,** 1120 SW Fifth Ave. Symbol of the city, *Portlandia* is the second-largest hammered bronze statue in the country, second only to the Statue of Liberty. The massive kneeling figure holds a trident in one hand and reaches toward the street with the other. This classically designed figure perches incongruously above the entrance to the controversial Portland Building, considered to be the first postmodern structure in the country. Today anyone familiar with the bizarre constructions of Los Angeles architect Frank Gehry would find it difficult to understand how such an innocuous and attractive building could have ever raised such a fuss, but it did just that in the early '80s.

Oregon Historical Society Museum ✸   In the middle of the 19th century, the Oregon Territory was a land of promise and plenty. Thousands of hardy individuals set out along the Oregon Trail, crossing a vast and rugged country to reach the fertile valleys of this region. Others came by ship around Cape Horn. If you'd like to learn about the people who discovered Oregon before you, visit this well-designed museum. Fascinating exhibits chronicle Oregon's history from before the arrival of the first Europeans to well into the 20th century. Museum docents, with roots stretching back to the days of the Oregon Trail, are often on hand to answer questions. You can't miss this museum—look for the eight-story-high *trompe l'oeil* mural stretching across the front.

1200 SW Park Ave. ⓒ **503/222-1741**. www.ohs.org. Admission $10 adults, $8 students and seniors, $5 children 6–18, free for children under 6. Mon–Sat 10am–5pm; Sun noon–5pm. Bus: 6 or 8. MAX: Library Station. Portland Streetcar: Art Museum (northbound); 11th Ave. and Jefferson St. (southbound).

Portland Art Museum 🏃🏃 This is the oldest art museum in the Northwest and in October 2005 it added a new wing that gave the museum lots more space for displaying its collection of modern and contemporary art. This collection begins with European Impressionist and moves right up to the present. Although the museum also has respectable collections of European, Asian, and American art, the best reason to visit is to see the extensive collection of Native American art and artifacts. There's also a good collection of Northwest contemporary art that includes a fascinating two-story wall of "artifacts" by glass artist William Morris. The Portland Art Museum is also frequently the Northwest stop for touring blockbuster exhibits. There's also a small sculpture court. October through April, on Wednesday nights from 5:30 to 7:30pm, the Museum After Hours program presents live music (admission is $8–$10 if you aren't a museum member). Between November 5, 2006, and March 4, 2007, there will be an exhibit of ancient Egyptian treasures.

1219 SW Park Ave. ⓒ **503/226-2811**. www.portlandartmuseum.org. Admission $10–$15 adults, $9–$13 seniors and students, $6 children 5–18, free for children under 5. Tues–Wed and Sat 10am–5pm; Thurs–Fri 10am–8pm; Sun noon–5pm. Bus: 6. MAX: Library Station. Portland Streetcar: Art Museum (northbound); 11th Ave. and Jefferson St. (southbound).

2 Skidmore Historic District, Chinatown & the Willamette River Waterfront

If Pioneer Courthouse Square is the city's living room, **Tom McCall Waterfront Park** 🏃, along the Willamette River, is the city's front yard play area. There are acres of lawns, shade trees, sculptures, and fountains, and the paved path through the park is popular with in-line skaters and joggers. This park also serves as the site of numerous festivals each summer. Also in the park is the Japanese-American Historical Plaza, dedicated to Japanese Americans who were sent to internment camps during World War II.

Just north of this plaza, a pedestrian walkway crosses the Steel Bridge to the east side of the Willamette River and the **Eastbank Esplanade,** which stretches for about 1½ miles along the east bank of the river. Although this paved multiuse path gets a lot of traffic noise from the adjacent freeway, it offers great views of the Portland skyline. Along the route there are small parks and gardens, interesting sculptures, and benches for sitting and soaking up the view. The highlight of this path is a section that floats right on the river and is attached to pilings in much the same way that a floating dock is constructed. You can access the Eastbank Esplanade by way of the pedestrian pathway on the Steel Bridge. This bridge is at the north end of Waterfront Park.

Oregon Maritime Center & Museum   This floating museum is housed in the historic steam-powered stern-wheeler *Portland,* which is docked at Tom McCall Waterfront Park. Inside the museum you'll find models of ships that once plied the Columbia and Willamette rivers. Also on display are early navigation instruments, artifacts from the battleship *Oregon,* old ship hardware, and other maritime memorabilia.

SW Pine St. and SW Naito Pkwy. (©) 503/224-7724. Admission $5 adults, $4 seniors, $3 youths 6–17, free for children under 6. Wed–Sun 11am–4pm. Bus: 12, 19, or 20. MAX: Skidmore Fountain Station.

Oregon Museum of Science and Industry (OMSI) 👎 (Kids) Located on the east bank of the Willamette River across from the south end of Waterfront Park, this modern science museum has six huge halls, and both kids and adults find the exhibits fun and fascinating. This is a hands-on museum, and everyone is urged to get involved with displays, from a discovery space for toddlers to physics and chemistry labs for older children. Simulated earthquakes and tornadoes are perennial favorites. There's plenty of pure entertainment at an **OMNIMAX theater** and the **Murdock Sky Theater,** which features laser-light shows and astronomy presentations. The USS *Blueback* submarine (used in the film *The Hunt for Red October*) is docked here, and tours are given daily.

A paved pathway runs beside OMSI and heads north to the Eastbank Esplanade and south 3 miles to Oaks Bottom amusement park. Along the pathway beside the museum, there are several interesting informational plaques about the history of Portland and its relationship to the Willamette River. OMSI is also the departure point for several different boat cruises up and down the Willamette River.

1945 SE Water Ave. (©) 800/955-6674 or 503/797-6674. www.omsi.edu. Museum or OMNIMAX $9 adults, $7 seniors and children 3–13; $5.50 submarine tours, planetarium shows, and matinee laser-light shows; $7.50 evening laser shows; discounted combination tickets available. Thurs 2pm until closing all tickets are 2-for-1. Mid-June to Labor Day daily 9:30am–7pm; Labor Day to mid-June Tues–Sun 9:30am–5:30pm. Closed Thanksgiving and Christmas. Bus: 4, 14, or 33.

Pearls in the Pearl District

The Pearl District has become Portland's hottest neighborhood, and in addition to all the restaurants, wine bars, and boutiques, there are some fun works of public art and a beautiful little park that looks like a small park in Paris.

Stroll through the tree-shaded parks of the North Park blocks, which form the eastern edge of the Pearl District; at the Burnside Street end of these parks you'll see a huge Chinese bronze elephant that was a gift from one of Portland's sister cities. A couple of blocks north of this elephant, watch for a bronze dog-bowl water fountain set in a checkerboard floor of stone. This odd sculpture was created by William Wegman, famous for his humorous photos of his dogs.

Right in the heart of the Pearl District, at the corner of Northwest Johnson Street and Northwest Tenth Avenue, you'll find Jamison Square, a park with an unusual wall-like cascading waterfall that fills a shallow pool. Around the graveled areas of the park, you'll find bistro chairs where you can sit and enjoy a latte from a nearby espresso bar. Be sure to notice the totem pole–inspired sculptures along the western edge of the park.

Portland Classical Chinese Garden ✿✿   This classically styled Chinese garden takes up an entire city block and is the largest of its type outside of China. The walls surrounding these gardens in Portland's Chinatown separate the urban 21st century from the timeless Chinese landscape within. The landscape is designed to evoke the wild mountains of China and to create a tranquil oasis within an urban setting. The gardens are centered on a small pond, which, at one end, has a rock wall meant to conjure up the sort of images often seen in Chinese scroll paintings. Numerous pavilions, a small bridge, and a winding pathway provide ever-changing views of the gardens. With its many paved paths and small viewing pavilions, this garden has a completely different feel than the Japanese Garden. Try to visit as soon as the gardens open in the morning; when the crowds descend and the guided tours start circulating—well, so much for tranquillity. On the other hand, if you want to learn more about the garden, you can join a guided tour at noon or 1pm. Be sure to stop and have a cup of tea and maybe a snack in the garden's tearoom.

NW Everett St. and NW 3rd Ave. ☏ 503/228-8131. www.portlandchinesegarden. org. Admission $7 adults, $6 seniors, $5.50 students and children 6–18, free for children 5 and under. Apr–Oct daily 9am–6pm; Nov–Mar daily 10am–5pm. Bus: 1, 4, 5, 8, 10, 16, 33, 40, or 77. MAX: Old Town/Chinatown Station.

Portland Saturday Market ☀ The Portland Saturday Market (actually held on both Sat and Sun) is arguably the city's best-loved event. For years the Northwest has attracted artists and craftspeople, and every Saturday and Sunday nearly 300 of them can be found selling their creations here. In addition to the dozens of crafts stalls, you'll find ethnic and unusual foods and lots of free entertainment. This is one of the best places in Portland to shop for one-of-a-kind gifts. The atmosphere is always cheerful and the crowds colorful. Located at the heart of the Skidmore District, Portland Saturday Market makes an excellent starting or finishing point for a walk around Portland's downtown historic neighborhood. On Sunday, on-street parking is free.

Underneath the west end of the Burnside Bridge between SW 1st Ave. and SW Naito Pkwy. ☏ 503/222-6072. www.portlandsaturdaymarket.com. Free admission. First weekend in Mar to Christmas Eve Sat 10am–5pm and Sun 11am–4:30pm. Bus: 12, 19, or 20. MAX: Skidmore Fountain Station.

3 Washington Park & Portland's West Hills

Portland is justly proud of its green spaces, and foremost among them are **Washington Park** and **Forest Park.**

Within Washington Park, you'll find the **Japanese Garden** and **International Rose Test Garden,** which are adjacent to one another on the more developed east side of the park (see the listings below). On the west side of the park (farther from the city center), you'll find not only the Hoyt Arboretum but also the Oregon Zoo, World Forestry Center Discovery Museum, and Portland Children's Museum.

The 185-acre **Hoyt Arboretum** (☏ 503/865-8733; www.hoyt arboretum.org) ☀ is planted with 1,100 species of trees and shrubs from temperate regions around the world and has several miles of hiking trails. Between April and October, there are free 1-hour guided tours of the arboretum on the first Saturday of the month at 10am. At the south end of the arboretum, adjacent to the World Forestry Center Discovery Museum and the Oregon Zoo, is the **Vietnam Veterans Living Memorial.** At the Visitor Center, 4000

SW Fairview Blvd. (open Mon–Fri 9am–4pm, Sat 9am–3pm), you can pick up maps and guides to the arboretum. The arboretum can be reached either from the Oregon Zoo/World Forestry Center Discovery Museum/Portland Children's Museum area or by following the arboretum signs from West Burnside Street.

To the north of Hoyt Arboretum is **Forest Park** 𝕽𝕽 (𝄢 **503/ 823-PLAY**), which, with more than 5,000 acres of forest, is the largest forested city park in the United States. Within the park, there are more than 74 miles of trails and old fire roads for hiking, jogging, and mountain biking. More than 100 species of birds call this forest home, making it a great spot for urban bird-watching. Along the forest trails, you can see huge old trees and find quiet picnic spots tucked away in the woods. One of the most convenient park access points is at the top of Northwest Thurman Street (just keep heading uphill until the road dead-ends). However, if you park at the Hoyt Arboretum Visitor Center (see above) or the Audubon Society (see below), you can pick up a map of Forest Park and head out from either of these locations.

Adjacent to Forest Park, you'll also find the **Portland Audubon Society,** 5151 NW Cornell Rd. (𝄢 **503/292-6855;** www.audubon portland.org), which has a couple of miles of hiking trails on its forested property. In keeping with its mission to promote enjoyment, understanding, and protection of the natural world, these nature trails are open to the public. You can also visit the Nature Store or Wildlife Care Center here. To find this facility from downtown Portland, first drive to Northwest 23rd Avenue and then head uphill on Northwest Lovejoy Street, which becomes Northwest Cornell Road. (*Warning:* Car break-ins are commonplace at the parking area just down the road from the Audubon Society, so don't leave anything of value in your car.)

By car, the easiest route to the Washington Park attractions from downtown Portland is to take Southwest Jefferson Street west, turn right onto Southwest 18th Avenue, turn left onto Southwest Salmon Street, turn right onto Southwest King Street, and then turn left onto Southwest Park Place. Although this sounds confusing, you'll find most of the route well marked with SCENIC DRIVE signs. Alternatively, you can drive west on West Burnside Street and watch for signs to the arboretum, or take the zoo exit off U.S. 26. All of these attractions can also be reached via bus no. 63. You can also take the MAX line to the Washington Park Station, which is adjacent to the Oregon Zoo, World Forestry Center Discovery Museum, Portland

Children's Museum, and Hoyt Arboretum. From here, it is possible (in the summer months) to take a bus shuttle to the Japanese Garden and International Rose Test Garden. There's also a miniature train that runs from the zoo to a station near the two public gardens. However, to ride this train, you must first pay zoo admission.

International Rose Test Garden ☞☞ Covering more than 5 acres of hillside in the West Hills above downtown Portland, these are among the largest and oldest rose test gardens in the United States and are the only city-maintained test gardens to bestow awards on each year's best roses. The gardens were established in 1917 by the American Rose Society and are used as a testing ground for new varieties of roses. Though you will probably see some familiar roses in the Gold Medal Garden, most of the 400 varieties on display are new hybrids being tested before marketing. Among the roses in bloom from late spring to early winter, you'll find a separate garden of miniature roses. There's also a Shakespeare Garden that includes flowers mentioned in the Bard's works. After seeing these acres of roses, you'll understand why Portland is known as the City of Roses and why the Rose Festival in June is the city's biggest

Great Photo Ops

If you've seen a photo of Portland with conical snow-covered Mount Hood looming in the background and you want to snap a similar photo while you're in town, there are several places to try. Most popular are probably the terraces of the International Rose Test Garden and from behind the pavilion at the Japanese Garden. Another great view can be had from the grounds of the Pittock Mansion. All three of these places are described in detail elsewhere in this chapter.

One other view is located atop Council Crest, a hilltop park in Portland's West Hills. To reach this park, take the Sylvan exit off U.S. 26 west of downtown Portland, turn south and then east (left) on Humphrey Boulevard, and then follow the signs. Alternatively, you can follow Southwest Broadway south out of downtown Portland and follow the signs. This road winds through attractive hillside neighborhoods for a ways before reaching Council Crest.

All Aboard!

The **Washington Park and Zoo Railway** travels between the zoo and the International Rose Test Garden and Japanese Garden. Tickets for the miniature railway are $3.50 for adults, $2.75 for seniors and children 3 to 11, and free for children under 3. There's also a shorter route that just loops around the zoo.

---

annual celebration. The small Rose Garden Store (© **503/227-7033**) is packed with rose-inspired products.

400 SW Kingston Ave., Washington Park. © **503/823-3636**. Free admission (donations accepted). Daily dawn–dusk. Bus: 63.

The Japanese Garden 𝕽𝕽𝕽   Considered the finest example of a Japanese garden in North America, Portland's Japanese Garden should not be missed. Not only are there five different styles of Japanese gardens scattered over 5½ acres, but there's also a view of volcanic Mount Hood, which has a strong resemblance to Mount Fuji.

Although Japanese gardens are traditionally not designed with colorful floral displays in mind, this garden definitely has its seasonal highlights. In early spring there are the cherry trees, in mid-spring there are the azaleas, in late spring a huge wisteria bursts into bloom, and in early summer huge Japanese irises color the banks of a pond. Among the gardens, there's a beautiful and very realistic waterfall.

This is a very tranquil spot and is even more peaceful on rainy days when the crowds stay away, so don't pass up a visit just because of inclement weather. Also, on the third Saturday of each of the summer months, there's a demonstration of the Japanese tea ceremony in the garden's teahouse.

611 SW Kingston Ave. (in Washington Park). © **503/223-1321**. www.japanese garden.com. Admission $6.75 adults, $5 seniors, $4 students and children 6–17, free for children under 6. Apr–Sept Mon noon–7pm; Tues–Sun 10am–7pm; Oct–Mar Mon noon–4pm, Tues–Sun 10am–4pm. Closed Thanksgiving, Christmas, and New Year's Day. Bus: 63. MAX: Washington Park Station (then, in summer months, take the shuttle bus or the zoo train).

Oregon Zoo 𝕽 𝓚𝓲𝓭𝓼   The Oregon Zoo is perhaps best known for its elephants and has the largest breeding herd of elephants in captivity. However, in recent years, the zoo has been adding new exhibits and branching out beyond the world of pachyderms. The Africa exhibit, which includes a very lifelike rainforest and a savanna populated by zebras, rhinos, giraffes, hippos, and other animals, is one of the most realistic habitats you'll ever see at a zoo. Equally impressive is the Alaskan tundra exhibit, with grizzly bears, wolves, and musk oxen. The Cascade Crest exhibit includes mountain goat habitat, and in the Steller Cove exhibit, you can watch the antics of Steller's sea lions and sea otters. Don't miss the bat house or the Amazon Flooded Forest exhibit.

In the summer, there are **outdoor concerts** in the zoo's amphitheater; admission prices vary.

4001 SW Canyon Rd., Washington Park. ✆ 503/226-1561. www.oregonzoo.org. Admission $9.50 adults, $8 seniors, $6.50 children 3–11, free for children under 2; $2 admission for all 2nd Tues of each month. Apr 15–Sept 15 daily 9am–6pm; Sept 16–Apr 14 daily 9am–4pm. Closed Christmas. Bus: 63. MAX: Washington Park Station.

Pittock Mansion ⟁ At nearly the highest point in the West Hills, 1,000 feet above sea level, stands the most impressive mansion in Portland. Once slated to be torn down to make way for new housing, this grand château, built by the founder of Portland's *Oregonian* newspaper, is fully restored and open to the public. Built in 1914 in a French Renaissance style, the mansion featured many innovations, including a built-in vacuum system and amazing multiple showerheads in the bathrooms. Today it's furnished with 18th- and 19th-century antiques, much as it might have been at the time the Pittocks lived here. With an expansive view over the city to the Cascade Range, the lawns surrounding the mansion are great for picnics. You can also access Forest Park's Wildwood Trail from here.

3229 NW Pittock Dr. ✆ 503/823-3624. www.pittockmansion.org. Admission $6 adults, $5 seniors, $3 children 6–18. June–Aug daily 11am–4pm; Sept–May daily noon–4pm. Closed 4 days in late Nov, Christmas, and the month of Jan.

World Forestry Center Discovery Museum ⟁ Although Oregon depends less and less on the timber industry with each passing year, this museum is still busy educating visitors about the importance of forest resources around the world. Step inside the huge wooden main hall, and come face to bark with several large and very lifelike trees. Press a button at its base and you can pilot a video camera around the tree's branches. Pay an extra few dollars, and you can climb into a chairlift that lets you explore these same trees. In another exhibit, you can practice being a smoke jumper (firefighter), while in another area you can go on a video raft ride. There are also interesting temporary exhibits staged here throughout the year, from photographic exhibits to displays of the woodworker's art.

4033 SW Canyon Rd. ✆ 503/228-1367. www.worldforestry.org. Admission $7 adults, $6 seniors, $5 children 5–18, free for children under 6. Daily 10am–5pm.

Closed Thanksgiving, Christmas Eve, and Christmas. Bus: 63. MAX: Washington Park Station.

4 Portland's Other Public Gardens

For Portland's two best-loved public gardens, the **International Rose Test Garden** and the **Japanese Garden,** see "Washington Park & Portland's West Hills," earlier in this chapter.

If roses are your passion, you'll also want to check out the **Peninsula Park Rose Garden** at the corner of North Portland Boulevard and North Albina Avenue (take the Portland Blvd. exit off I-5 and go 2 blocks east), which has even more rose bushes than the International Rose Test Garden.

The Berry Botanic Garden ☞   Originally founded as a private garden, the Berry Botanic Garden is now one of Portland's favorite public gardens. Among the highlights is a large, forestlike collection of mature rhododendron shrubs. There are also rock gardens with unusual plants, a native plant trail, and a fern garden. The garden is open by reservation only.

The World's Smallest Park

Don't blink as you cross the median strip on Naito Parkway at the corner of Southwest Taylor Street, or you might just walk right past **Mill Ends Park,** the smallest public park in the world.

Covering a whopping 452 square inches of land, this park was the whimsical creation of local journalist Dick Fagen. After a telephone pole was removed from the middle of Naito Parkway (then known as Front Ave.), Fagen dubbed the phone pole hole Mill Ends Park (Mill Ends, a lumber mill term, was the name of Fagen's newspaper column). The columnist, whose office looked down on the hole in the middle of Front Avenue, peopled the imaginary park with leprechauns and would often write of the park's goings-on in his column. On St. Patrick's Day 1976, it was officially designated a Portland city park. Rumor has it that despite its diminutive size, the park has been the site of several weddings (although the parks department has never issued a wedding permit for it).

11505 SW Summerville Ave. ⓒ 503/636-4112. www.berrybot.org. Adults $5. Open daylight hours by appointment. Bus: 35.

Crystal Springs Rhododendron Garden ⍟   Nowhere do rhododendrons do better than in the cool, rainy Northwest, and nowhere in Portland is there a more impressive planting of rhodies than at Crystal Springs. Eight months out of the year, this is a tranquil garden, with a waterfall, a lake, and ducks to feed. But when the rhododendrons and azaleas bloom from March to June, it becomes a spectacular mass of blazing color. The Rhododendron Show and Plant Sale is held here on Mother's Day weekend.

SE 28th Ave. (1 block north of SE Woodstock Blvd.). ⓒ 503/771-8386. Admission $3 Mar 1 to Labor Day Thurs–Mon 10am–6pm; free at other times. Open year-round daily dawn–dusk. Bus: 19.

Elk Rock Garden of the Bishop's Close ⍟   Set on a steep hillside above the Willamette River between Portland and Lake Oswego, this was once a private garden but was donated to the local Episcopal bishop of Oregon on the condition that it be opened to the public. The mature gardens are at their best through the spring and early summer. There's also an excellent view of Mount Hood from the grounds.

11800 SW Military Lane. ⓒ 800/452-2562 or 503/636-5613. www.diocese-oregon. org/theclose. Free admission. Daily 8am–5pm. Bus: 35.

5 Especially for Kids

In addition to the attractions listed below, the kids will especially enjoy the **Oregon Museum of Science and Industry** (p. 82), which has lots of hands-on exhibits, and the **Oregon Zoo** (p. 87). From inside the zoo, it's possible to take a small train through Washington Park to the International Rose Test Garden, below which there is the **Rose Garden Children's Park,** a colorful play area for younger children. The **Salmon Street Springs fountain,** in downtown's Tom McCall Waterfront Park (at SW Naito Pkwy. and SW Salmon St.), is another fun place to take the kids. During hot summer months, there are always lots of happy kids playing in the jets of water that erupt from the pavement here. There are also big lawns in **Waterfront Park,** so the kids can run off plenty of excess energy. There's also a splashy play-pond at Jamison Square in the Pearl District.

Oaks Park Amusement Center (Kids)   What would summer be without the screams of happy thrill-seekers risking life and limb on a roller coaster? Covering more than 44 acres, this amusement park first opened in 1905 to coincide with the Lewis and Clark Exposition. Beneath the shady oaks for which the park is named, you'll find waterfront picnic sites, miniature golf, music, and plenty of thrilling rides. Check out the largest wood-floored roller-skating rink in the west, where an organist still plays the Wurlitzer for the skaters.

East end of the Sellwood Bridge. (C) **503/233-5777**. www.oakspark.com. Free admission; individual-ride tickets $1.75; limited-ride bracelet $11; deluxe-ride bracelet $14. Rides open Apr to early Oct; skating rink open year-round. Hours vary seasonally; call for details. Bus: 40.

Portland Children's Museum ⟲ *Kids*   Located across the parking lot from the Oregon Zoo, this large, modern children's museum includes exhibits for children from 6 months to 13 years. Kids can act out fairy tales, play in a magical forest, or go shopping in a kid-size grocery store. However, it is the Water Works exhibit that is likely to make the biggest splash with your kids. There are also six studios with changing exhibits and opportunities for exploring the visual, literary, and performing arts. Combined with the nearby zoo, this museum makes for an easy all-day kid-oriented outing.

4015 SW Canyon Rd. (C) **503/223-6500**. www.portlandcm2.org. Admission $6 adults and children, $5 seniors, free for children under 1 year. Tues–Sat 9am–5pm; Sun 11am–5pm. Closed some national holidays. Bus: 63. MAX: Washington Park Station.

6 Organized Tours

CRUISES

With two large rivers winding through the city, Portland is a town that needs to be seen from the water. Try the *Portland Spirit* ((C) **800/224-3901** or 503/224-3900; www.portlandspirit.com), a 75-foot yacht that specializes in dinner cruises. Lunch, brunch, and dinner cruises feature Northwest cuisine with views of the city skyline. There are also basic sightseeing cruises, and on Friday nights July through September, there are also Friday afternoon cocktail cruises with a live band. Call for reservations and schedule. Prices range from $16 to $60 for adults, and $11 to $55 for children. This company also operates jet-boat tours that go up the Columbia River to the Bonneville Dam and down the Columbia to Astoria.

For high-speed tours up the Willamette River, there are the **Willamette Jetboat Excursions** ⟲ ((C) **888/538-2628** or 503/231-1532; www.willamettejet.com). These high-powered open-air boats blast their way from downtown Portland to the impressive

Willamette Falls at Oregon City. The 2-hour tours, which start at OMSI, are $29 for adults and $19 for children 4 to 11, free for children 3 and under. Tours are offered from late April to early October. There are also less expensive 1-hour tours, but these do not go upriver to the falls.

BUS TOURS

If you want to get a general overview of Portland, **Gray Line** (© 888/684-3322 or 503/243-6789; www.grayline.com) offers several half-day and full-day tours. One itinerary takes in the International Rose Test Garden and Pittock Mansion; another stops at the Portland Classical Chinese Garden and the Pearl District. There are also tours to see the waterfalls in the Columbia Gorge, to Mount Hood, and to the Oregon coast. Tour prices range from $34 to $75 for adults, and from $17 to $38 for children.

RAIL EXCURSIONS

While Portland is busy reviving trolleys and streetcars as a viable mass-transit option, the **Willamette Shore Trolley** ⊕ (© 503/697-7436; www.trainweb.org/oerhs/wst.htm) offers scenic excursions along the Willamette River in historic trolley cars (including a double-decker) from the early part of this century. The old wooden trolleys rumble over trestles and through a tunnel as they cover the 7 miles between Portland and the upscale suburb of Lake Oswego (a 40-min. trip). Along the way, you pass through shady corridors with lots of views of the river and glimpses into the yards of posh riverfront homes. In Lake Oswego, the trolley station is on State Street, between A Avenue and Foothills Road. In Portland, the station is about 1 mile south of downtown in an industrial area off Macadam Avenue at the corner of Moody Avenue and Bancroft Street. The round-trip fare is $10 for adults, $9 for seniors, and $6 for children 3 to 12. Call for a schedule.

WALKING TOURS

Peter's Walking Tours of Portland (© 503/665-2558; www.walk portland.com), led by Peter Chausse, are a great way to learn more about Portland. The walking tours of downtown take 3 hours and take in the city's fountains, parks, historic places, art, and architecture. Tours are by reservation and cost $15 for adults and $5 teens (free for children 7 and under with a paying adult).

Two to three times a year, Sharon Wood Wortman, author of *The Portland Bridge Book,* offers a **Bridge Tour** that explores several Portland bridges. These tours are offered through the Outdoor

Recreation Program of **Portland Parks and Recreation** (© 503/
823-5132; www.portlandparks.org). Many other walking tours are
also available through Portland Parks and Recreation.

The seamy underbelly of history is laid bare on **Portland Underground Tours** ⚑ (© 503/622-4798; www.members.tripod.com/
cgs-mthood), which head down below street level in the historic
Old Town neighborhood. On these unusual tours, which are only
for those who are steady on their feet and able to duck under pipes
and joists and such, you'll hear tales of the days when Portland was
known as one of the most dangerous ports on the Pacific Rim.
Sailors were regularly shanghaied from bars and brothels in this area,
and a vast network of tunnels and underground rooms was developed to support the shanghaiing business. Tours cost $12 for adults
and $7 for children under 12, and are offered by reservation only.

WINERY TOURS

If you're interested in learning more about Oregon wines, contact
Grape Escape (© 503/283-3380; www.grapeescapetours.com),
which offers in-depth winery tours of the Willamette Valley. All-day
tours include stops at several wineries, appetizers, lunch, and
dessert, and pickup and drop-off at your hotel ($95–$165 per person). For people with less time, there are half-day afternoon trips
that take in two or three wineries ($75–$125 per person).

For information on touring wine country on your own, see
"Winery Tours," p. 93.

7 Outdoor Pursuits

If you're planning ahead for a visit to Portland, contact **Metro,** 600
NE Grand Ave., Portland, OR 97232-2736 (© 503/797-1850;
www.metro-region.org/parks), for its *Metro GreenScene* publication
that lists tours, hikes, classes, and other outdoor activities and events
being held in the Portland metro area.

BIKING

Portland is a very bicycle-friendly city, and you'll notice plenty of
cyclists on the streets. There are also miles of paved bike paths
around the city and some good mountain biking areas as well. For
mountain-bike rentals, head to **Fat Tire Farm,** 2714 NW Thurman
St. (© 503/222-3276), where bikes go for $25 to $50 a day.
Straight up Thurman Street from this bike shop, you'll find the trail
head for **Leif Erikson Drive,** an old gravel road that is Forest Park's

favorite route for cyclists and runners (the road is closed to motor vehicles); the trail is 12 miles long.

If you'd like to explore Portland's riverfront bike paths, stop in at **Waterfront Bicycle Rentals,** 0315 SW Montgomery St., Suite 360 (© **503/227-1719**), where you can rent a bike for $7.50 to $13 per hour or $26 to $35 per half-day. From here head through Tom McCall Waterfront Park, cross the Steel Bridge, and ride down the Eastbank Esplanade path. This trail leads 4 miles south to the upscale Sellwood neighborhood.

GOLF

If you're a golfer, don't forget to bring your clubs along on a trip to Portland. There are plenty of public courses around the area, and greens fees at municipal courses range from $23 to $40 for 18 holes. Municipal golf courses operated by the Portland Bureau of Parks and Recreation include **Redtail Golf Course,** 8200 SW Scholls Ferry Rd. (© **503/646-5166**); **Eastmoreland Golf Course,** 2425 SE Bybee Blvd. (© **503/775-2900**), which is the second-oldest golf course in the state (this one gets our vote for best municipal course); **Heron Lakes Golf Course,** 3500 N. Victory Blvd. (© **503/289-1818**), which has two courses designed by Robert Trent Jones; and **Rose City Golf Course,** 2200 NE 71st Ave. (© **503/253-4744**), on the site of a former country club. For more information, log on to **www.parks.ci.portland.or.us/Parks/golf.htm**.

If you want to tee off where the pros play, head west from Portland 20 miles to **Pumpkin Ridge Golf Club** *৻৻*, 12930 NW Old Pumpkin Ridge Rd., North Plains (© **503/647-4747**; http://pumpkin ridge.nemexinc.com), a 36-hole course that has hosted the U.S. Women's Open. Greens fees range from $30 to $150 on the one course that is open to the public.

Also west of the city, on the south side of Hillsboro, you'll find **The Reserve Vineyards and Golf Club** *৻৻*, 4805 SW 229th Ave., Aloha (© **503/649-8191**; www.reservegolf.com). Greens fees range from $40 to $85, depending on time of year and day of the week.

HIKING

Hiking opportunities abound in the Portland area. For shorter hikes, you don't even have to leave the city; just head to **Forest Park.** Bordered by West Burnside Street on the south, Newberry Road on the north, St. Helens Road on the east, and Skyline Road on the west, this is the largest forested city park in the country. Within this urban wilderness, you'll find more than 50 miles of trails. One of our favorite access points is at the top of Northwest Thurman Street in northwest Portland. (After a hike, you can stop by one of the neighborhood brewpubs, an espresso bar, or a bakery along NW 23rd or NW 21st aves. for a post-exercise payoff.) The Wildwood Trail is the longest trail in the park and along its length offers lots of options for loop hikes. For a roughly 2.5-mile hike, head up Leif Erickson Drive to a left onto the Wild Cherry Trail, to a right onto the Wildwood Trail, to a right onto the Dogwood Trail, and then a right onto Leif Erickson Drive to get you back to the trail head. There are also good sections of trail to hike in the vicinity of the Hoyt Arboretum. To reach the arboretum's visitor center, 4000 SW Fairview Blvd. (open Mon–Fri 9am–4pm and Sat 9am–4pm), drive west on West Burnside Street from downtown Portland and follow signs to the arboretum. You can get a trail map here at the visitor center.

About 5 miles south of downtown, you'll find **Tryon Creek State Park** on Terwilliger Boulevard. This park is similar to Forest Park and is best known for its displays of trillium flowers in the spring. There are several miles of walking trails within the park, and a bike path to downtown Portland starts here.

You can buy or rent camping equipment from **REI Co-Op,** 1405 NW Johnson St. (② **503/221-1938**). This huge outdoor-recreation-supply store also sells books on hiking in the area.

SEA KAYAKING

If you want to check out the Portland skyline from water level, arrange for a sea kayak tour through the **Portland River Company** ☆☆ , 0315 SW Montgomery St., Suite 330 (② **888/238-2059** or 503/229-0551; www.portlandrivercompany.com), which operates out of the RiverPlace Marina at the south end of Tom McCall Waterfront Park. A 2½-hour tour that circles nearby Ross Island costs $43 to $47 per person. This company also rents sea kayaks (to experienced paddlers) for $10 to $20 per hour.

SKIING

There are several ski resorts on the slopes of Mount Hood within about an hour's drive of Portland. Timberline Ski Area even boasts summer skiing. There are also many miles of marked cross-country ski trails. The best cross-country skiing on Mount Hood is at the Nordic center at Mount Hood Meadows, and at Teacup Lake, which is along Highway 35 near the turnoff for Mount Hood Meadows. You'll find numerous ski and snowboard rental shops in the town of Sandy, which is on the way from Portland to Mount Hood, and ski areas also rent equipment.

Timberline Ski Area ✻ (© **503/222-2211;** www.timberline lodge.com) is the highest ski area on Mount Hood and has one slope that is open all the way through summer. This is the site of the historic Timberline Lodge, which was built during the Depression by the WPA. Adult lift ticket prices range from $20 for night skiing to $46 for an all-day pass. Call for hours of operation.

Mount Hood Meadows ✻✻ (© **800/SKI-HOOD;** 503/227-7669 for snow report; www.skihood.com), 12 miles northeast of Government Camp on Oregon 35, is the largest ski resort on Mount Hood, with more than 2,000 skiable acres, 2,777 vertical feet, five high-speed quad lifts, and a wide variety of terrain. This is the closest Mount Hood comes to having a destination ski resort, and consequently, it is here that you'll find the most out-of-state skiers. Lift ticket prices range from $22 for night skiing to $52 for a peak-season all-day pass. Call for hours of operation.

Mt. Hood SkiBowl (© **503/272-3206;** 800/754-2695 or 503/222-2695 for snow report; www.skibowl.com), located in Government Camp on U.S. 26, the closest ski area to Portland, offers 1,500 vertical feet of skiing and has more expert slopes than any other ski area on the mountain. SkiBowl is also one of the largest lighted ski areas in the country. Adult lift ticket prices range from $30 to $36 for an all-day pass. Call for hours of operation.

All of the ski areas mentioned above allow snowboarding. Mount Hood Meadows and Mt. Hood SkiBowl both have cross-country skiing (though only Mount Hood Meadows has a Nordic Center and groomed fee-access trails).

TENNIS

Portland Parks and Recreation operates more than 120 tennis courts, both indoors and out, all over the city. Outdoor courts are generally free and available on a first-come, first-served basis. My personal favorites are those in Washington Park just behind the International Rose Test Garden. If you want to be certain of getting a particular court time, some of these courts can be reserved by contacting Portland Parks and Recreation at © **503/823-2525.**

If the weather isn't cooperating, head for the **Portland Tennis Center,** 324 NE 12th Ave. (© **503/823-3189**). They have indoor courts and charge $20 for 1¼ hours.

WHITE-WATER RAFTING

The Cascade Range produces some of the best white-water rafting in the country, and the White Salmon, Sandy, and Clackamas rivers all offer plenty of rafting opportunities within an hour or two of Portland. The Sandy and the Clackamas are the two closest rivers.

Portland River Company, 0315 SW Montgomery St. (© **888/ 238-2059** or 503/229-0551; www.portlandrivercompany.com), offers day trips on the Deschutes River ($79 per person). Trips on the Sandy, Clackamas, North Santiam, and Hood rivers are offered by **Blue Sky Whitewater Rafting** (© **800/898-6398** or 503/630-3163; www.blueskyrafting.com), which charges $45 to $65 for a half-day trip and $70 to $95 for a full-day trip. **River Drifters** (© **800/972-0430**; www.riverdrifters.net) offers trips on the Sandy, White Salmon, Deschutes, Clackamas, Wind, North Santiam, and Klickitat rivers for between $70 and $95 for a full day. **Zoller's Outdoor Odysseys, Inc.** (© **800/366-2004** or 509/493-2641; www.zooraft.com) offers half-day trips on the White Salmon for $60 and all-day trips on the Klickitat for $85.

8 Spectator Sports

Tickets to most games, including those of the Trail Blazers and the Portland Beavers, are sold through **Ticketmaster** (© **503/224-4400**; www.ticketmaster.com).

Tickets to events at the Rose Garden arena and Memorial Coliseum are also sold through the **Rose Quarter** box office (© **503/ 797-9617**; www.rosequarter.com). The Rose Garden arena is home to the Portland Trail Blazers and is the main focal point of Portland's **Rose Quarter.** This sports and entertainment neighborhood includes the Rose Garden, Memorial Coliseum, and several restaurants and bars. To reach the Rose Garden or adjacent Memorial Coliseum, take the Rose Quarter exit off I-5. Parking is expensive, so you might want to consider taking the MAX light-rail line from downtown Portland (the Rose Quarter stop is in the Fareless Sq.).

AUTO RACING   **Portland International Raceway,** West Delta Park, 1940 N. Victory Blvd. (© **503/823-RACE;** www.portlandraceway.com), hosts road races, drag races, motorcross and other motorcycle races, go-kart races, and even vintage-car races. February through October are the busiest months here.

BASEBALL   The **Portland Beavers Baseball Club** (© **503/553-5400** or 503/224-4400 for tickets; www.portlandbeavers.com), the

AAA affiliate of the San Diego Padres, plays minor-league ball at PGE Park, Southwest 20th Avenue and Morrison Street. Tickets are $7 to $12.

BASKETBALL The NBA's **Portland Trail Blazers** (© **503/231-8000** or 503/797-9619; www.nba.com/blazers) do well enough each year to have earned them a very loyal following. Unfortunately, they have a habit of not quite making it all the way to the top. The Blazers pound the boards at the Rose Garden arena. Call for current schedule and ticket information. Tickets are $10 to $131. If the Blazers are doing well, you can bet that tickets will be hard to come by.

9 Day Spas

If you'd rather opt for a massage than a hike in the woods, consider spending a few hours at a day spa. These facilities typically offer massages, facials, seaweed wraps, and the like. Portland day spas include the **Avalon Hotel & Spa,** 0455 SW Hamilton Ct. (© **503/802-5800**); **Aveda Lifestyle Store and Spa,** 5th Avenue Suites Hotel, 500 Washington St. (© **503/248-0615**); and **Salon Nyla—The Day Spa,** adjacent to the Embassy Suites hotel at 327 SW Pine St. (© **503/228-0389;** www.salonnyla.com). However, the most unusual day spas in town are in the Pearl District. **Nirvana Apothecary & Day Spa,** 736 NW 11th Ave. (© **503/546-8155;** www.nirvanadayspa.com), is done up sort of like a Moroccan palace, while **Aequis,** 419 SW 11th Ave. (© **503/223-7847;** www.aequisspa.com), is an Asian-inspired retreat that follows Ayurvedic principles. Expect to pay about $85 or $95 for a 1-hour massage and $200 to $450 for a multi-treatment spa package.

7

Walking Tour of Portland

Portland's compactness makes it an ideal city to explore on foot. There's no better way to gain a feel for this city than to stroll through the Skidmore Historic District, into Tom McCall Waterfront Park, and over to the hip and bustling Pearl District. If you're here on the weekend, you'll also be able to visit the Portland Saturday Market. For additional information on several stops in this stroll, see chapter 6, "Exploring Portland."

WALKING TOUR	CHINATOWN, OLD TOWN & THE PEARL DISTRICT

Start:	Portland Classical Chinese Garden.
Finish:	Powell's City of Books.
Time:	Allow approximately 4 to 5 hours, including breaks and shopping stops.
Best Times:	Saturday and Sunday between March and December, when the Portland Saturday Market is open; start early in the day so you can visit the Chinese Garden before the crowds arrive.
Worst Times:	After dark, when the Skidmore neighborhood is not as safe as in daylight.

Every decade or so Portland hits on some great idea for reinventing its inner city. Back in the 1970s, it was the removal of a highway so a park could be built along the Willamette River waterfront. In the 1980s, it was the preservation of the Skidmore Historic District (Old Town), the city's last remaining 19th-century downtown commercial neighborhood. In the late 1990s and early 2000s, an area of northwest Portland that consisted of old warehouses and a sprawling railroad yard became the new frontier. Now known as the Pearl District, this latter area has become the hottest real estate in the city and is frequently flaunted as an example of how cities can do things right by creating urban villages. After starting out in the city's small Chinatown, this walking tour meanders through the above-mentioned neighborhoods, which showcase more than a century of Portland urban living.

Begin your walking tour at the corner of Northwest Everett Street and Northwest Third Avenue at the:

❶ Portland Classical Chinese Garden

This is the largest classical Suzhou-style Chinese garden outside of China. With its tiled roofs, pond, bridges, and landscaping that conjures up images from Chinese scroll paintings, the garden is an urban oasis. See p. 83.

If it's a Saturday or Sunday between March and December, walk east on Northwest Everett Street to Northwest First Avenue and turn right. In 3 blocks, you'll likely spot the crowds of people under the Burnside Bridge at the:

❷ Portland Saturday Market

Here you'll find a wide variety of crafts by Northwest artisans. There typically are nearly 300 artisans plus entertainers and food vendors, and though a lot of what's sold here these days tends to be cheap gifts, there are still plenty of quality vendors of fine crafts. See p. 84.

Adjacent to the Portland Saturday Market, at the corner of Southwest Naito Parkway and Southwest Ankeny Street, you can check out some vintage fire-fighting equipment at the:

❸ Jeff Morris Memorial Fire Museum

This little museum houses several horse-drawn steamers from the early part of the 20th century. Because the museum is part of an active fire station and because the equipment is packed so tightly together, you can't actually go inside. You'll have to be satisfied with looking through the glass doors that face the street.

Continue 2 blocks south on Southwest Naito Parkway to Southwest Pine Street and cross the street to:

❹ Gov. Tom McCall Waterfront Park

This long swath of green fronts the Willamette River and was once the site of a highway. Today the park hosts summertime festivals and is a popular place for jogging, bicycling, and strolling by the river. If you're a serious power walker and want to add an extra 3 miles of walking to this tour, you can walk a loop around the Willamette by crossing over to the Eastbank Esplanade on the Steel Bridge (at the north end of Waterfront Park) and then returning to the west bank via the Hawthorne Bridge.

Just about the first thing you'll see when you enter Waterfront Park is the:

❺ Oregon Maritime Center and Museum

This floating museum is housed in the stern-wheeler *Portland* and is dedicated to Oregon's shipping history. Walk down the gangplank, and you can take a tour of this old paddle-wheeler.

Walking Tour: Chinatown, Old Town & the Pearl District

1 Portland Classical Chinese Garden
2 Portland Saturday Market
3 Jeff Morris Memorial Fire Museum
4 Gov. Tom McCall Waterfront Park
5 Oregon Maritime Center and Museum
6 Skidmore Fountain
7 New Market Block

8 The North Park Blocks
9 Quintana Gallery
10 Ecotrust's Jean Vollum Natural Capital Center
11 Jamison Square
12 Powell's City of Books

Now backtrack to the Saturday Market, and at the corner of Southwest First Avenue and Southwest Ankeny Street, you'll find the:

6 Skidmore Fountain

Erected in 1888, the fountain was intended to provide refreshment for "horses, men, and dogs," and it did that for many years. Today, however, the bronze-and-granite fountain is primarily decorative.

Across Southwest First Avenue is the:

7 New Market Block

Constructed in 1872 to house the unlikely combination of a produce market and a theater, the New Market Block contains some unusual shops and budget restaurants, as do many of the restored historic buildings in this area. The free-standing wall of archways extending out from the New Market Building was salvaged from an

Old Town structure that didn't survive the urban renewal craze of the 1960s.

Now walk north on Southwest First Avenue, go under the Burnside Bridge, continue to Northwest Couch Street (it's pronounced Kooch), and turn left. Continue up Northwest Couch Street to Northwest Eighth Avenue, where you'll find:

⑧ The North Park Blocks

These shady blocks are among the prettiest parks in downtown Portland. In the block between Northwest Couch and West Burnside streets, you'll see a large Chinese bronze elephant sculpture that was donated to the city. If you then walk north through the Park Blocks to the Northwest Park Avenue side of the parks between Northwest Davis and Northwest Everett streets, you'll come across one of the most unusual sculptures/fountains in the city. The *Portland Dog Bowl* was created by celebrated dog photographer William Wegman and consists of a bronze dog-bowl water fountain on a stone checkerboard-patterned "floor."

Now walk back to Northwest Davis Street and turn right. At the next corner, Northwest Ninth Avenue, turn left, and in the middle of the block, at 120 NW Ninth Ave., you'll find:

⑨ Quintana Gallery

You simply won't find a better selection of Northwest Coast Native American art than at this little gallery. There are both traditional and contemporary pieces, and Native American artists from outside the Northwest are also represented.

TAKE A BREAK
Even if you haven't yet worked up an appetite, stop at **Pearl Bakery,** 102 NW Ninth Ave. (✆ **503/827-0910**). Don't pass up an opportunity to sample the pastries at this classic little bakery on the edge of the Pearl District.

Now continue west to Northwest 10th Avenue and turn right. In 6 blocks, at the corner of Northwest 10th Avenue and Northwest Irving Street, you'll find one of the most unusual buildings in the Pearl District:

⑩ Ecotrust's Jean Vollum Natural Capital Center

Located at 721 NW Ninth Ave., this building looks from Northwest Ninth Avenue like any other Portland historic building. However, the facade facing Northwest 10th Avenue is a merger of historic building and modern architecture, and what you can't see are all the environmentally aware "green" building techniques that were used in the renovation of this building. Today the building is home to environmental and other nonprofit organizations. You'll also find a Patagonia store, a pizza counter, and an espresso bar.

Diagonally across the intersection from the Ecotrust building is:

⑪ Jamison Park

With its crushed rock plaza, wooden sidewalk, benches, and bistro tables, this little park looks as though it could have been transported from some neighborhood in Paris. Although this is a great place to just sit in the sun and read a book, it is particularly popular with families, who let the kids play in the park's unusual pondlike water feature, which has a long waterfall wall along one side.

If you exit this park on Northwest 11th Avenue, you will be on one of the best shopping streets in the Pearl District. Between Northwest Irving and Northwest Hoyt streets, you'll find numerous small boutiques. Continue along Northwest 11th Avenue to Northwest Couch Street, where you'll find:

⑫ Powell's City of Books

This massive bookstore has long been Portland's favorite hangout for the literate, and schedules frequent author appearances and book signings. You can easily spend hours perusing the three floors of books here. If your energy level flags, you can get a light meal or espresso in the bookstore's cafe. When it's time to leave, you can hop on the Portland Streetcar, which stops right outside the store. If you ride the streetcar into downtown, you don't even have to pay.

8

Shopping

Portland has no sales tax, making it a popular shopping destination for Washingtonians, who cross the Columbia River to avoid paying their state's substantial sales tax.

1 The Shopping Scene

The **blocks around Pioneer Courthouse Square** are the heartland of upscale shopping in Portland. It's here that you'll find Nordstrom, NIKETOWN, Saks Fifth Avenue, Tiffany, Pioneer Place shopping mall, and numerous upscale boutiques and shops.

However, Portland's hippest shopping districts are the **Pearl District** and **Nob Hill/Northwest,** both of which are in northwest Portland. Most of the Pearl District's best shopping is along Northwest 10th and 11th avenues going north from West Burnside Street. Here you'll find all kinds of trendy boutiques, art galleries, and home-furnishing stores. The best Nob Hill shopping is along Northwest 23rd Avenue going north from West Burnside Street. Both neighborhoods have block after block of interesting, hip boutiques and, along Northwest 23rd Avenue, a few national chains such as Gap, Urban Outfitters, and Pottery Barn.

For shops with a more down-to-earth, funky flavor, head out to the **Hawthorne District,** which is the city's counterculture shopping area (lots of tie-dye and imports).

Most small stores in Portland are open Monday through Saturday from 9 or 10am to 5 or 6pm. Shopping malls are usually open Monday through Friday from 9 or 10am to 9pm, Saturday from 9 or 10am to between 6 and 9pm, and Sunday from 11am until 6pm. Many department stores stay open past 6pm. Most art galleries and antiques stores are closed on Monday.

2 Shopping A to Z

ANTIQUES

The **Sellwood** neighborhood (south of downtown at the east end of the Sellwood Bridge) is Portland's main antiques-shopping district, with about 30 antiques shops and antiques malls along 12 blocks of Southeast 13th Avenue. With its old Victorian homes and 19th-century architecture, Sellwood is an ideal setting for these shops. There are plenty of good restaurants in the area, in case it turns into an all-day outing.

You'll also find three more large antiques malls (all under the same ownership) nearby on Milwaukie Boulevard: **Stars,** at 6717 SE Milwaukie Blvd. (© **503/235-9142**), and at 7027 SE Milwaukie Blvd. (© **503/239-0346**); and **Star & Splendid,** 7030 SE Milwaukie Blvd. (© **503/235-5990**).

ART GALLERIES

On the **first Thursday of the month,** galleries in downtown Portland schedule coordinated openings in the evening. Stroll from one gallery to the next, meeting artists and perhaps buying an original work of art. On the last Thursday of each month, galleries in the Northeast Alberta Street neighborhood stage a similar event. This latter event tends to attract a very culturally diverse crowd and has become the hottest art scene in the city. To find Northeast Alberta Street, drive north from downtown Portland on I-5 and watch for the Northeast Alberta Street exit.

A guide listing dozens of Portland galleries is available at galleries around the city.

GENERAL ART GALLERIES

Augen Gallery   When it opened nearly 20 years ago, the Augen Gallery focused on internationally recognized artists such as Jim Dine, Andy Warhol, and David Hockney. Today the gallery has expanded its repertoire to regional contemporary painters and printmakers. 817 SW 2nd Ave. © **503/224-8182.** www.augengallery.com.

Blackfish Gallery   Artist-owned since 1979, the Blackfish is a large space featuring contemporary images. Since this gallery is a cooperative, it doesn't have the same constraints as a commercial art gallery and thus can present more cutting-edge and thought-provoking work. 420 NW 9th Ave. © **503/224-2634.** www.blackfish.com.

The Laura Russo Gallery   The focus here is on Northwest contemporary artists, showcasing talented emerging artists as well as the estates of well-known regional artists. Laura Russo has been on the Portland art scene for a long time and is highly respected. 805 NW 21st Ave. © **503/226-2754.** www.laurarusso.com.

Pulliam Deffenbaugh Gallery   This gallery represents a long list of both talented newcomers and masters from the Northwest. Solo shows and salon-style group shows are held here. 929 NW Flanders St. ✆ **503/228-6665.** www.pulliamdeffenbaugh.com.

Quintana Galleries   This large, bright space is virtually a small museum of Native American art, selling everything from Northwest Indian masks to contemporary paintings and sculptures by various Northwest-coast Indian and Inuit artists. They also carry a smattering of Northwest and Southwest Indian antiquities. The jewelry selection is outstanding. Prices, however, are not cheap. 120 NW 9th Ave. ✆ **800/321-1729** or 503/223-1729. www.quintanagalleries.com.

ART GLASS
The Bullseye Connection   Located in the Pearl District, the Bullseye Connection is a large open exhibition and sales space for glass artists. Pieces sold here include sculptures, delightful glass jewelry, paperweights, and even marbles. There's even a Dale Chihuly chandelier of pink fruitlike objects on display. Workshops and lectures related to glassmaking are also offered. The **Bullseye Connection Gallery,** which is across the street at 300 NW 13th St. (✆ **503/ 227-0222**), shows work of internationally acclaimed glass artists. 1308 NW Everett St. ✆ **503/227-2797.** www.bullseye-glass.com.

BOOKS
Major chain bookstores in Portland include **Barnes & Noble,** 1720 Jantzen Beach Center (✆ **503/283-2800**), and **Borders,** 708 SW Third Ave. (✆ **503/220-5911**). For information on Portland's massive Powell's City of Books, see the box below.

CRAFTS
For the largest selection of local crafts, visit the **Portland Saturday Market** (see "Markets," below), which is a showcase for local crafts.

Contemporary Crafts Museum & Gallery   In business since 1937 and located in a residential area between downtown and the John's Landing neighborhood, this is the nation's oldest nonprofit art gallery showing exclusively artwork in clay, glass, fiber, metal, and wood. The bulk of the large gallery is taken up by glass and ceramic pieces in ongoing thematic exhibitions. There are also several cabinets of jewelry. 3934 SW Corbett Ave. ✆ **503/223-2654.** www. contemporarycrafts.org.

Hoffman Gallery   The Hoffman Gallery is on the campus of the Oregon College of Art and Craft, one of the nation's foremost crafts

The City of Books

Portland's own **Powell's City of Books,** 1005 W. Burnside St. (✆ **503/228-4651** or 866/201-7601; www.powells.com), is the bookstore to end all bookstores. Powell's, which covers an entire city block three floors deep, claims to be the world's largest bookstore. At any given time, the store has roughly three-quarters of a million books on the shelves. Both new and used books are shelved side by side, which is why browsing is what Powell's is all about.

Once inside the store, be sure to pick up a store map, which will direct you to the color-coded rooms. Serious book collectors won't want to miss a visit to the Rare Book Room. *One warning:* If you haven't got at least an hour of free time, enter at your own risk. It's so easy to lose track of time at Powell's that many customers miss meals and end up in the store's in-house cafe.

Believe it or not, City of Books is even bigger than what you see here; it has several satellite stores, including **Powell's Technical Books,** 33 NW Park St. (✆ **503/228-3906**); **Powell's Books for Cooks and Gardeners,** 3747 SE Hawthorne Blvd. (✆ **503/235-3802**); **Powell's Books on Hawthorne,** 3723 SE Hawthorne Blvd. (✆ **503/238-1668**); and **Powell's Books at PDX,** Portland International Airport (✆ **503/249-1950**).

education centers since 1906. The gallery hosts installations and group shows by local, national, and international artists. The adjacent gift shop has a good selection of handcrafted items. The grounds are serene and relaxing, and there is also a cafe. **8245 SW Barnes Rd.** ✆ **503/297-5544.**

The Real Mother Goose This is Portland's premier fine crafts shop and one of the top such shops in the United States. It showcases only the very best contemporary American crafts, including imaginative ceramics, colorful art glass, intricate jewelry, exquisite wooden furniture, and sculptural works. Hundreds of craftspeople and artists from all over the United States are represented here. **901 SW Yamhill St.** ✆ **503/223-9510.** www.therealmothergoose.com. Also at Washington Square, Tigard (✆ **503/620-2243**), and Portland International Airport, Main Terminal (✆ **503/284-9929**).

Twist This large store has quite a massive selection of wildly colorful and imaginative furniture, crockery, glassware, and lamps, and also a limited but impressive selection of handmade jewelry from artists around the United States. 30 NW 23rd Place. ✆ 503/224-0334. www.twistonline.com. Also at Pioneer Place, 700 SW Fifth Ave. (✆ 503/222-3137).

DEPARTMENT STORES

Meier and Frank Meier and Frank is a Portland institution and has been doing business here for more than 100 years. The flagship store on Pioneer Courthouse Square was built in 1898 and, with 10 stories, was at one time the tallest store in the Northwest. Today those 10 floors of consumer goods and great sales still attract crowds of shoppers. Prices are lower than at nearby Nordstrom. 621 SW 5th Ave. ✆ 503/223-0512. Also at 1100 Lloyd Center (✆ 503/281-4797) and 9300 SW Washington Square Rd. in Tigard (✆ 503/620-3311).

Nordstrom Directly across the street from Pioneer Courthouse Square and a block away from Meier and Frank, Nordstrom is a top-of-the-line department store that originated in Seattle and takes great pride in its personal service and friendliness. 701 SW Broadway. ✆ 503/224-6666. Also at 1001 Lloyd Center (✆ 503/287-2444) and 9700 SW Washington Square Rd. in Tigard (✆ 503/620-0555).

FASHION
MEN'S & WOMEN'S

Langlitz Leathers This family-run shop produces the Harley Davidson of leather jackets. Even though there may be a wait (the shop turns out only six handmade jackets a day), motorcyclists ride their Harleys all the way from the East Coast to be fitted. 2443-A SE Division St. ✆ 503/235-0959.

Norm Thompson Known throughout the country for its mail-order catalogs, Norm Thompson is a mainstay of the well-to-do in Portland. Classic styling for men and women is the name of the game here. 1805 NW Thurman St. ✆ 503/221-0764. Also at Portland International Airport (✆ 503/249-0170). www.normthompson.com.

Portland Outdoor Store In business since 1919, this Western-wear store is a Portland institution that feels little changed from decades ago. The big neon sign out front and the old general-store atmosphere is enough to pull in even people who aren't into playing cowboy or cowgirl. 304 SW 3rd Ave. ✆ 800/222-1051 or 503/222-1051.

The Portland Pendleton Shop Pendleton wool is as much a part of life in the Northwest as forests and salmon. This company's fine wool fashions for men and women define the country-club look in the Northwest and in many other parts of the country. Pleated skirts and tweed jackets are de rigueur here, as are the colorful blankets that have warmed generations of Northwesterners through long, chilly winters. 900 SW 5th Ave. (entrance is actually on 4th Ave. between Salmon and Taylor). ✆ **800/241-9665** or 503/242-0037.

SPORTSWEAR

Columbia Sportswear Company   This flagship store is surprisingly low-key, given that the nearby Nike flagship store and REI in Seattle are designed to knock your socks off. Displays showing Columbia Sportswear's well-made outdoor clothing and sportswear are rustic, with lots of natural wood. The most dramatic architectural feature of the store is the entryway, in which a very wide tree trunk seems to support the roof. 911 SW Broadway. ✆ **503/226-6800.**

Columbia Sportswear Company Factory Outlet Store *Value* This outlet store in the Sellwood neighborhood south of downtown and across the river sells remainders and past-season styles from the above-mentioned sportswear company, which is one of the Northwest's premier outdoor clothing manufacturers. You'll pay 30% to 50% less here than you will at the downtown flagship store. 1323 SE Tacoma St. ✆ **503/238-0118.**

Nike Factory Company Store *Value*   The Nike outlet is one season behind the current season at NIKETOWN (see below), selling swoosh brand running, aerobic, tennis, golf, basketball, kids, and you-name-it sports clothing and accessories at discounted prices. 2650 NE Martin Luther King Jr. Blvd. ✆ **503/281-5901.**

NIKETOWN Portland   Sure, you may have a NIKETOWN back home, but this one is the closest to Nike's headquarters in nearby Beaverton, which somehow makes it just a little bit special. A true shopping experience. 930 SW 6th Ave. ✆ **503/221-6453.**

WOMEN'S CLOTHING

Changes   This shop specializes in handmade clothing, including hand-woven scarves, jackets, shawls, handpainted silks, and other wearable art. 927 SW Yamhill St. ✆ **503/223-3737.**

FOOD

The **Made in Oregon** shops offer the best selection of local food products. See "Gifts & Souvenirs," below, for details.

GIFTS & SOUVENIRS

For unique locally made souvenirs, your best bet is the **Portland Saturday Market** (see "Markets," below, for details).

Made in Oregon   This is your one-stop shop for all manner of made-in-Oregon gifts, food products, and clothing. Every product sold is either grown, caught, or made in Oregon. You'll find smoked salmon, filberts, jams and jellies, Pendleton woolens, and Oregon wines. All branches are open daily, but hours vary from store to store. 921 SW Morrison St. (in the Galleria). © **800/828-9673** or 503/241-3630. www.madeinoregon.com. Also at Portland International Airport (© **503/282-7827**) and in Lloyd Center mall, SE Multnomah St. and SE Broadway (© **503/282-7636**).

JEWELRY

For some of the most creative jewelry in Portland, visit **Twist,** the **Hoffman Gallery,** the **Contemporary Crafts Gallery,** and the **Real Mother Goose.** See "Crafts," above.

MALLS & SHOPPING CENTERS

Pioneer Place   Just a block from Pioneer Courthouse Square, this is Portland's most upscale shopping center. Anchored by a Saks Fifth Avenue, Pioneer Place is filled with stores selling designer fashions and expensive gifts. 700 SW 5th Ave. (between 3rd and 5th aves.). © **503/228-5800.** www.pioneerplace.com.

MARKETS

Portland Saturday Market   The Portland Saturday Market (held on both Sat–Sun) is a Portland tradition. Every weekend nearly 300 artists and craftspeople can be found selling their creations at this open-air market beneath the Burnside Bridge. In addition to the dozens of crafts stalls, you'll find ethnic and unusual foods, and lots of free entertainment. This is one of the best places in Portland to shop for one-of-a-kind gifts that are small enough to fit into your suitcase. On Sunday, on-street parking is free. Under the west end of the Burnside Bridge (between SW 1st Ave. and SW Naito Pkwy.). © **503/222-6072.** www.portlandsaturdaymarket.com. Open from the 1st weekend in Mar to Christmas Eve, Sat 10am–5pm, Sun 11am–4:30pm; closed Jan–Feb.

TOYS

Finnegan's Toys and Gifts   This is the largest toy store in downtown Portland and appeals to the kid in all of us. It'll have your inner child kicking and screaming if you don't buy that silly little toy you never got when you were young. 922 SW Yamhill St. © **503/221-0306.** www.finneganstoys.com.

WINE

Oregon Wines on Broadway   This cozy wine bar/shop is located diagonally across from the Hotel Vintage Plaza in downtown Portland. Here you can taste some of Oregon's fine wines, including 30 different pinot noirs, as well as chardonnays, Gewürztraminers and Washington State cabernet sauvignons, merlots, and Syrahs. 515 SW Broadway. ℂ **800/943-8858** or 503/228-4655. www.oregon winesonbroadway.com.

9

Portland After Dark

Portland is the Northwest's number two cultural center (after Seattle, of course). The city's symphony orchestra, ballet, and opera are all well regarded, and the many theater companies offer classic and contemporary plays. In summer, festivals move the city's cultural activities outdoors.

To find out what's going on during your visit, pick up a copy of *Willamette Week*, Portland's free weekly arts-and-entertainment newspaper. The *Oregonian*, the city's daily newspaper, also publishes lots of entertainment-related information in its Friday "A&E" section and also in the Sunday edition of the paper.

1 The Performing Arts

For the most part, the Portland performing-arts scene revolves around the **Portland Center for the Performing Arts (PCPA),** 1111 SW Broadway (© **503/248-4335;** www.pcpa.com), which is comprised of five performance spaces in three different buildings. The **Arlene Schnitzer Concert Hall,** known locally as the Schnitz, at Southwest Broadway and Southwest Main Street, is an immaculately restored 1920s movie palace that still displays the original Portland theater sign and marquee out front and is home to the Oregon Symphony. This hall also hosts popular music performers, lecturers, and many other special performances. Directly across Main Street from the Schnitz, at 1111 SW Broadway, is the sparkling glass jewel box known as the **New Theater Building.** This building houses both the **Newmark** and **Dolores Winningstad** theaters and **Brunish Hall.** The Newmark Theatre is home to Portland Center Stage, while the two theaters together host stage productions by local and visiting companies. Free tours of all three of these theaters are held Wednesdays at 11am, Saturdays every half-hour between 11am and 1pm, and the first Thursday of every month at 6pm.

A few blocks away from this concentration of venues is the 3,000-seat **Keller Auditorium,** Southwest Third Avenue and Southwest Clay Street, the largest of the four halls and the home of the Portland

Opera and the Oregon Ballet Theatre. The auditorium was constructed shortly after World War I and completely remodeled in the 1960s. In addition to the resident companies mentioned above, these halls host numerous visiting companies each year, including touring Broadway shows.

The PCPA's box office is open for ticket sales Monday through Saturday from 10am to 5pm. Tickets to PCPA performances, and also performances at many other venues around the city, are also sold through either **Ticketmaster** (© 503/224-4400; www.ticketmaster. com), which has outlets at area G.I. Joe's and Fred Meyer stores, or **Tickets West** (© 800/992-8499 or 503/224-8499; www.tickets west.com), which has outlets at area Safeway stores. The PCPA does, however, have a **Half-Price Ticket Hotline** (© 503/275-8358) that sells day-of-show, half-price tickets to theater performances by some of the area's smaller companies.

One other performing arts venue worth checking out is **The Old Church,** 1422 SW 11th Ave. (© 503/222-2031; www.oldchurch. org). Built in 1883, this wooden Carpenter Gothic church is a Portland landmark. It incorporates a grand, traditional design but was constructed with spare ornamentation. Today the building serves as a community facility, and every Wednesday at noon it hosts free lunchtime organ recitals on the church's 1883 organ. There are also many other performances held here throughout the year.

DANCE

Although the **Oregon Ballet Theatre** (© 888/922-5538 or 503/ 222-5538; www.obt.org), which performs at the Keller Auditorium and the Newmark Theatre (see above), is best loved for its performances of *The Nutcracker* each December, the rest of each season includes performances of classic and contemporary ballets (tickets $13–$66).

Fans of modern dance should be sure to check to see what's being staged by **White Bird** (© 503/245-1600; www.whitebird.org). This organization brings in such celebrated companies as Twyla Tharp Dance, the Merce Cunningham Dance Company, the Paul Taylor Dance Company, and the Alvin Ailey American Dance Theater.

Also keep an eye out for performances by **Imago Theatre,** 17 SE Eighth Ave. (© 503/231-9581; www.imagotheatre.com), which, though it is also a live theater company, is best known for its wildly creative productions of *Frogz* and *Big Little Things,* both of which are fanciful dance performances that appeal to both adults and children. **Do Jump! Extremely Physical Theatre** (© 503/231-1232;

www.dojump.org) is another highly creative dance company worth watching for. Their performances incorporate dance, acrobatics, aerial work, and plenty of humor.

OPERA & CLASSICAL MUSIC

Founded in 1896, the **Oregon Symphony** (© 800/228-7343 or 503/228-1353; www.orsymphony.org), which performs at the Arlene Schnitzer Concert Hall, 1111 SW Broadway (see above), is the oldest symphony orchestra on the West Coast and is currently under the baton of conductor Carlos Kalmar. Each year between September and June, the symphony stages several series, including classical, pops, Sunday matinees, and children's concerts. Ticket prices range from $7 to $85 (seniors and students may purchase half-price tickets 1 hr. before concerts).

Each season, the **Portland Opera** (© 866/739-6737 or 503/241-1802; www.portlandopera.org), which performs at Keller Auditorium, Southwest Third Avenue and Southwest Clay Street (see above), offers five different productions that include both grand opera and light opera. The season runs November through May. Ticket prices range from $37 to $145.

Summer is the time for Portland's annual chamber music binge. **Chamber Music Northwest** (© 503/294-6400; www.cmnw.org) is a 5-week-long series that starts in late June and attracts the world's finest chamber musicians. Performances are held at Reed College and Catlin Gable School (tickets $21–$40).

PERFORMING ARTS SERIES

The **Museum After Hours** series at the **Portland Art Museum,** 1219 SW Park Ave. (© 503/226-2811; www.portlandartmuseum.org), is a great place to catch some of the best local jazz, blues, rock, and folk bands. Performances are held October through April on Wednesday nights from 5:30 to 7:30pm, and admission is $8 if you aren't a museum member.

When summer hits, Portlanders like to head outdoors to hear music. The city's top outdoor music series is held at **Oregon Zoo,** 4001 SW Canyon Rd. (© 503/226-1561; www.oregonzoo.org), which brings in the likes of the Indigo Girls, Gipsy Kings, Pink Martini, and John Hiatt. Ticket prices range from $9.50 to $26.

THEATER

Portland Center Stage (© 503/274-6588; www.pcs.org), which holds performances at the Portland Center for the Performing Arts,

1111 SW Broadway (see above), is Portland's largest professional theater company. They stage a combination of six to seven classic and contemporary plays during their September-to-April season (tickets $20–$51).

Portland's other main theater company, **Artists Repertory Theatre,** 1516 SW Alder St. (✆ **503/241-1278;** www.artistsrep.org), often stages more daring plays. They can be hit-or-miss, but they're frequently very thought provoking. The season often includes a world premiere. Tickets run $15 to $40.

If it's musicals you want, you've got a couple of options in Portland. At the Keller Auditorium, you can catch the **Broadway in Portland** series (✆ **503/241-1802;** www.broadwayacrossamerica. com). Tickets range from around $30 to $135.

2 The Club & Music Scene

CABARET

Darcelle's XV   In business since 1967 and run by Portland's best-loved cross-dresser, this cabaret is a campy Portland institution with a female-impersonator show that has been a huge hit for years. There are shows Wednesday through Saturday. 208 NW 3rd Ave. ✆ 503/ 222-5338. www.darcellexv.com. Cover $10. Reservations recommended.

DANCE CLUBS

See also the listing for **Saucebox,** below, under "Bars"; this restaurant and bar becomes a dance club after 10pm, when a DJ begins spinning tunes.

Andrea's Cha-Cha Club   Located in the Grand Cafe and open Wednesday through Saturday nights, this is Portland's premier dance spot for fans of Latin dancing. Whether it's cha-cha, salsa, or the latest dance craze from south of the border, they'll be doing it here. Lessons are available Wednesday and Friday nights at 9pm. 832 SE Grand Ave. ✆ 503/230-1166. Cover $2–$3.

JAZZ

The Blue Monk on Belmont   Conjuring up images of the famous Blue Note jazz club and Thelonious Monk, this little jazz club in southeast Portland is a neo-bohemian hangout that books a wide range of jazz acts. 3341 SE Belmont St. ✆ 503/595-0575. www.the bluemonk.com. Cover free–$5.

Imbibe ✿   With live jazz and other types of adult music most nights of the week, this bar/dinner club is one of the most enjoyable places in Portland to take in some live music. The musical bookings are very eclectic, so be sure to check the schedule when you're in town. 2229 SE Hawthorne Blvd. ℂ 503/239-4002. www.takeitin.com. Cover free–$5.

Jimmy Mak's This small Pearl District club is one of Portland's last remaining jazz clubs. *Downbeat* magazine even ranked it as one of the top 100 jazz clubs in the country. Monday through Saturday nights, there's live music. Okay, so sometimes it's blues music, but I won't hold that against them. 300 NW 10th Ave. ℂ 503/295-6542. Cover free–$25.

The Lobby Court Hands down the most elegant old-world bar in Portland, the Lobby Court is in the city's most luxurious hotel, The Benson. The Circassian walnut paneling and crystal chandeliers will definitely put you in the mood for a martini or single malt. Tuesday through Sunday, there's live jazz in the evening. In The Benson Hotel, 309 SW Broadway. ℂ 503/228-2000.

ROCK, BLUES & FOLK

Aladdin Theater This former movie theater now serves as one of Portland's main venues for touring performers such as Richard Thompson, Bruce Cockburn, Judy Collins, and They Might Be Giants. The very diverse musical spectrum represented includes blues, rock, ethnic, country, folk, and jazz. 3017 SE Milwaukie Ave. ℂ 503/233-1994. www.aladdin-theater.com. Tickets $10–$35.

Berbati's Pan Located in Old Town, this has long been one of Portland's best and most popular rock clubs. A wide variety of acts play here, primarily the best of the local rock scene and bands on the verge of breaking into the national limelight. Be sure to check out the back bar, which is 150 years old. 10 SW 3rd Ave. ℂ 503/226-2122. Cover $5–$15.

Crystal Ballroom The Crystal Ballroom first opened before 1920 and since then has seen performers ranging from early jazz musicians to James Brown, Marvin Gaye, and the Grateful Dead. The McMenamin Brothers (of local brewing fame) renovated the Crystal Ballroom several years back and refurbished its dance floor, which, due to its mechanics, feels as if it's floating. The ballroom now hosts a variety of performances and special events nearly every night of the week. **Lola's Room,** a smaller version of the Ballroom, is on the second floor and also has a floating dance floor. You'll find **Ringlers Pub** (a colorful brewpub) on the ground floor. 1332 W. Burnside St. ℂ 503/225-0047. www.danceonair.com. Cover free–$30.

Doug Fir Lounge With a no-smoking policy and shows that are usually over by midnight, this bar may not sound like too much fun, but it is, in fact, the hottest club in Portland. The decor is an incongruous blend of log cabin and Swedish modern, but somehow it all works. 830 E. Burnside St. © 503/231-9663. Cover $5–$20.

Roseland Theater & Grill The Roseland Theater, though it isn't all that large, is currently one of Portland's two or three main venues for performances by touring national rock acts. Be sure to check the schedule; you never know who might be playing. 8 NW 6th Ave. © 503/224-2038. Cover $5–$35.

3 The Bar & Pub Scene

BARS

Bartini Located just off Northwest 21st Avenue, this dark little bar specializes in, you guessed it, martinis. In fact, they've got a list of more than 100 martinis on offer. Good happy hour. 2108 NW Glisan St. © 503/224-7919.

The Brazen Bean This hip cocktail and cigar bar in an old Victorian home in northwest Portland has a cool *fin de siècle* European elegance that makes it a very classy place to sip a martini. This is mainly a man's domain, but cigar-puffing women will appreciate it as well. 2075 NW Glisan St. © 503/294-0636.

Huber's No night out on the town in Portland is complete until you've stopped in at Huber's for a Spanish coffee. These potent pick-me-ups are made with rum, Kahlúa, Triple Sec, coffee, and cream, and the preparation of each drink is an impressive show. 411 SW 3rd Ave. © 503/228-5686. www.hubers.com.

Jake's Famous Crawfish In business since 1892, Jake's is a Portland institution and should not be missed (see the full review on p. 61). The bar is one of the busiest in town when the downtown offices let out. 401 SW 12th Ave. © 503/226-1419. www.jakesfamouscrawfish.com.

McCormick and Schmick's Harborside Pilsner Room Located at the south end of Tom McCall Waterfront Park overlooking the Willamette River and RiverPlace Marina, this restaurant/bar is affiliated with Hood River's Full Sail brewery and keeps plenty of Full Sail brews on tap (plus other area beers). The crowd is upscale, the view one of the best in town. (See p. 61 for a review of the restaurant.) 0309 SW Montgomery St. © 503/220-1865. www.mccormickandschmicks.com.

Mint/820 Mixologist Lucy Brennan, owner of this swanky place, has single-handedly turned Portland into a town full of cocktail

Portland's Brewing Up a Microstorm

Espresso may be the drink that drives Portland, but when it's time to relax and kick back, **microbrewed beer** is often the beverage of choice around these parts. No other city in America has as large a concentration of brewpubs, and it was here that the craft-brewing business got its start in the mid-1980s. Today brewpubs can be found throughout the city, with cozy neighborhood pubs vying for business with big, polished establishments.

To fully appreciate what the city's craft brewers are concocting, it helps to have a little beer background. Beer has **four basic ingredients:** malt, hops, yeast, and water. The first of these, **malt,** is made from grains, primarily barley and wheat, which are roasted to convert their carbohydrates into the sugar needed to grow yeast. The amount of roasting the grains receive during the malting process determines the color and flavor of the final product. The darker the malt, the darker and more flavorful the beer or ale. There is a wide variety of malts, each providing its own characteristic flavor. **Yeast,** in turn, converts the malt's sugar into alcohol; there are many different strains of yeast that all lend different characters to beers. The **hops** are added to give beer its characteristic bitterness. The more "hoppy" the beer or ale, the more bitter it becomes. The Northwest is the nation's only commercial hop-growing region, with 75% grown in Washington and 25% grown in Oregon and Idaho.

Lagers, which are cold-fermented, are the most common beers in America and are made from pale malt with a lot of

connoisseurs. Using fresh fruit juices and purées and unusual ingredients, Brennan reinvented the cocktail into something deserving of quality ingredients. How about a beet-infused martini or a creamy avocado cocktail? 816/820 N. Russell St. © **503/284-5518.**

¡Oba!   One of the trendiest bars in Portland, this big Pearl District bar/nuevo Latino restaurant has a very tropical feel despite the warehouse district locale. After work, the bar is always packed with the stylish and the upwardly mobile taking advantage of great happy hour deals. Don't miss the tropical-fruit margaritas! 555 NW 12th Ave. © **503/228-6161.** www.obarestaurant.com.

hops added to give them their characteristic bitter flavor. **Pilsner,** a style of beer that originated in the mid–19th century in Czechoslovakia, is a type of lager. **Ales,** which are the most common brews served at microbreweries, are made using a warm fermentation process and usually with more and darker malt than is used in lagers and pilsners. **Porters** and **stouts** get their characteristic dark coloring and flavor from the use of dark, even charred, malt.

To these basics, you can then add a few variables. **Fruit-flavored beers,** which some disparage as soda-pop beer, are actually an old European tradition and, when considering the abundance of fresh fruits in the Northwest, are a natural here. Also immensely popular in Portland are **hefeweizen** (German-style wheat beer), which has a cloudy appearance, and **IPA (India pale ale),** which is strong and hoppy. If you see a sign for **nitro beer** in a pub, it isn't referring to their explosive brews—it means they've got a keg charged with nitrogen instead of carbon dioxide. The nitrogen gives the beer an extra-creamy head. (A nitro charge is what makes Guinness Stout so distinctive.) **Cask-conditioned ales,** served almost room temperature and with only their own carbon dioxide to create the head, are also popular. Although some people find these latter brews flat, others appreciate them for their unadulterated character.

It all adds up to a lot of variety in Portland pubs. Cheers!

Portland City Grill   Located way up on the 30th floor, this restaurant/bar has the best view in downtown Portland. Come for the great happy hour so you can catch the sunset, or stop by later in the night to catch some live jazz and check out the upscale singles scene. Unico/U.S. Bank Tower, 111 SW 5th Ave. ✆ **503/450-0030.** www.portland citygrill.com.

Saucebox   Popular with the city's dressed-in-black scene-makers, this recently remodeled downtown restaurant-bar is a large, dramatically lit dark box that can be very noisy. If you want to talk, you'd better do it before 10pm, when the DJ arrives to transform this place from restaurant/bar into dance club. Great cocktails. 214 SW Broadway. ✆ 503/241-3393. www.saucebox.com.

Vault Martini   No need for a combination or secret code to get into this Vault, but it does help to dress the part when drinking at this trendy Pearl District bar. The decor is sleek and stylish, and the cocktail menu is lengthy. 226 NW 12th Ave. ✆ 503/224-4909.

BREWPUBS

Although brewpubs have now become commonplace throughout much of the country, here in Portland they're still brewing beers the likes of which you won't taste in too many other places on this side of the Atlantic. This is the heart of the Northwest craft-brewing explosion, and if you're a beer connoisseur, you owe it to yourself to go directly to the source.

Brewpubs have become big business in Portland, and there are now glitzy upscale pubs as well as funky warehouse-district locals. No matter what vision you have of the ideal brewpub, you're likely to find your dream come true. Whether you're wearing bike shorts or a three-piece suit, there's a pub in Portland where you can enjoy a handcrafted beer, a light meal, and a convivial atmosphere.

With almost three dozen brewpubs in the Portland metropolitan area, the McMenamins chain is Portland's biggest brewpub empire. The owners of this empire think of themselves as court jesters, mixing brewing fanaticism with a Deadhead aesthetic. Throw in a bit of historic preservation and a strong belief in family-friendly neighborhood pubs, and you'll understand why these joints are so popular.

DOWNTOWN

McMenamin's Ringlers Pub   With mosaic pillars framing the bar, Indonesian antiques, and big old signs all around, this cavernous place is about as eclectic a brewpub as you'll ever find. A block away (at 1223 SW Stark St.) are the two associated pubs of Ringlers Annex, which is in a flat-iron building. One of these pubs is below street level with a beer cellar feel, and the other has walls of multipaned glass. These three pubs get my vote for most atmospheric alehouses in town. 1332 W. Burnside St. ✆ 503/225-0627. www.mcmenamins.com.

NORTHWEST PORTLAND

MacTarnahan's Tap Room   With huge copper fermenting vats proudly displayed and polished to a high sheen, this is by far the city's most ostentatious, though certainly not its largest, brewpub.

This pub's flagship brew, Mac's Scottish-style amber ale, has some very loyal local fans. 2730 NW 31st Ave. ℂ 503/228-5269.

Rogue Ales Public House   This Pearl District pub is an outpost of a popular microbrewery headquartered in the Oregon coast community of Newport. Rogue produces just about the widest variety of beers in the state and, best of all, keeps lots of them on tap at this pub. If you're a fan of barley-wine ale, don't miss their Old Crustacean. 1339 NW Flanders St. ℂ 503/222-5910.

SOUTHEAST

The Lucky Labrador Brew Pub   With a warehouse-size room, industrial feel, and picnic tables on the loading dock out back, this brewpub is a classic southeast Portland local. The crowd is young, and dogs are welcome. (They don't even have to be Labs.) 915 SE Hawthorne Blvd. ℂ 503/236-3555. www.luckylab.com.

Roots Brewing Co.   In keeping with Portland's granola-crunchy reputation, this little brewpub is the state's first all-organic brewery. The decor is industrial funky, and the clientele tends toward neohippies and dreadlocked students from nearby Reed College. Rest assured, though, that the beers are good. 1520 SE 7th Ave. ℂ 503/235-7668. www.rootsorganicbrewing.com.

NORTHEAST & NORTH PORTLAND

Alameda Brewhouse   With its industrial chic interior, this high-ceilinged neighborhood pub brews up some of the most unusual beers in Portland. How about a rose-petal bock, a juniper berry porter, or a heather-flower ale made without hops? Some work, some don't, but fans of craft beers have to appreciate the willingness to experiment. 4765 NE Fremont St. ℂ 503/460-9025. www.alamedabrewhouse.com.

Amnesia Brewing Company   With the look of an old warehouse and a "beer garden" in the parking lot, this little north Portland brewpub is another of Portland's old-school brewpubs, which means laid-back in the extreme. The beers are good beers, but the food is pretty limited. 832 N. Beech St. ℂ 503/281-7708.

McMenamin's Kennedy School   Never thought they'd ever start serving beer in elementary school, did you? However, in the hands of the local McMenamins brewpub empire, an old northeast Portland school is now a sprawling complex complete with brewpub, beer garden, movie theater pub, and even a bed-and-breakfast inn. Order up a pint and wander the halls checking out all the cool artwork. 5736 NE 33rd Ave. ℂ 503/249-3983. www.mcmenamins.com.

Widmer Brewing and Gasthaus   Located on the edge of a rapidly reviving industrial area just north of the Rose Garden arena, this place has the feel of a classic blue-collar pub. This is the brewery for Portland's largest craft-brewing company, which is best known for its hefeweizen. German and American foods are served. On the MAX Yellow Line. 955 N. Russell St. ⓒ **503/281-3333**. www.widmer.com.

WINE BARS

Bar Pastiche   This tiny little wine bar is attached to an upscale grocery store and is known for its diverse array of tiny tapas plates. While other tapas places around town feed you big little plates, this place serves little, little plates, but, boy, are they creative. The desserts, from Pix Patisserie, are works of art. 3731 SE Hawthorne Blvd. ⓒ **503/236-4760**.

Noble Rot   With a garage door for a front wall, this stylish little wine bar opens up to the fresh air whenever the weather is conducive. You can get various wine flights (selections of 2-oz. tastings), and there are plenty of Oregon wines available. The wine bar also serves excellent food. By the way, *noble rot* is a type of grape fungus that is utilized in the production of sweet dessert wines. 2724 SE Ankeny St. ⓒ **503/233-1999**. www.noblerot.biz.

Oregon Wines on Broadway   With just a handful of stools at the bar and a couple of cozy tables, this tiny place is the best spot in Portland to learn about Oregon wines. On any given night there

Blend Your Own Wine

Tired of wines that just don't do it for you? Always looking for a little more fruit and a little less tannin? Why not bottle up your own personal cuvee? At **Urban Wineworks**, 407 NW 16th Ave. (ⓒ **503/226-9797**; www.urbanwineworks.com), at the corner of Northwest Flanders Street, that's exactly what you get to do on Tuesday evenings between 6:30 and 7:30pm. You don't get to ferment the wine or manage the vineyard, but blending your own wine is both fun and educational. This winery also has a tasting room and wine bar, and on the first Thursday of every month between 5:30 and 8:30pm, they have artists paint an original work of art on the end of a wine barrel.

will be 30 Oregon pinot noirs available by the glass, and plenty of white wines as well. 515 SW Broadway. © 800/943-8858 or 503/228-4655. www.oregonwinesonbroadway.com.

Southpark Seafood Grill & Wine Bar   With its high ceiling; long, heavy drapes; halogen lights; and lively wall mural, the wine bar at Southpark (see the full dining review on p. 62) is a contemporary interpretation of a Parisian cafe from the turn of the last century. Very romantic. 901 SW Salmon St. © 503/326-1300.

Vino Paradiso   Located in the heart of the Pearl District, this is currently Portland's swankiest wine bar and has live music as well as lots of good wines. There are also some tasty menu items to go with your wine. 417 NW 10th Ave. © 503/295-9536.

Wine Down   Much more casual than nearby Noble Rot, this wine bar has live music and tends to attract a less style-conscious clientele. Still, you can get as snobby as you want with your wine. You'll find only a handful of Oregon wines on the list here. 126 NE 28th St. © 503/236-9463.

4 The Gay & Lesbian Nightlife Scene

BARS

The area around the intersection of **Southwest Stark Street and West Burnside Street** has the largest concentration of gay bars in Portland.

C.C. Slaughters Nightclub & Lounge   Popular with a young crowd, this Old Town bar spins disco sounds most nights, with a night of country music each week. 219 NW Davis St. © 503/248-9135. www.ccslaughterspdx.com.

Crush Bar   This big, hip bar is over in southeast Portland and attracts a very diverse crowd that includes not only gay men, but lesbians and straights as well. There are three distinct settings within the walls of this place, including a comfortable lounge, a room for dining and dancing, and a room where smoking is allowed. DJs spin dance tunes most nights. 1400 SE Morrison St. © 503/235-8150. www.crush bar.com.

Eagle Bar   If leather and Levi's are your uniform, then you'll feel right at home at this bar. Loud rock and DJ dance music plays most nights, and Sundays are currently leather night. 1300 W. Burnside St. © 503/241-0105. www.portlandeagle.com.

Moments   A Portland Original: The Theater Pub

Portland brewpub magnates the McMenamin brothers have a novel way to sell their craft ales—in movie pubs. Although it's often hard to concentrate on the screen, it's always a lot of fun to attend a show. The movies are usually recent releases that have played the main theaters but have not yet made it onto video. Theaters include the **Bagdad Theater,** 3702 SE Hawthorne Blvd. (*©* 503/236-9234), a restored classic Arabian Nights movie palace; the **Mission Theater,** 1624 NW Glisan St. (*©* 503/223-4527), which was the first McMenamins theater pub; the **Kennedy School Theater,** 5736 NE 33rd Ave. (*©* 503/249-3983), in a former elementary school; and the **Edgefield Theater,** 2126 SW Halsey St., Troutdale (*©* 503/669-8610). You can also have beer and pizza with your movie at the **Laurelhurst Theater,** 2735 E. Burnside St. (*©* 503/232-5511; www.laurelhursttheater.com), which is not a McMenamins establishment.

Scandal's & The Otherside Lounge   In business for more 25 years, this bar/restaurant is at the center of the gay bar scene. There always seems to be some special event going on here. Try to get a window seat so you can keep an eye on passersby on the sidewalk. 1038 SW Stark St. *©* **503/227-5887.**

A DANCE CLUB

The Embers Avenue   Though primarily a gay disco, Embers is also popular with straights. There are always lots of flashing lights and sweaty bodies until the early morning. Hip-hop and '90s pop are the current DJ faves. Look for drag shows several nights a week. 110 NW Broadway. *©* **503/222-3082.** Cover–$2–$5.

10

Side Trips from Portland

Portland likes to boast about how close it is to both the mountains and the beach, and no visit would be complete without a trip or two to the coast or the Cascades. Within a 90-minute drive, you can be walking on a Pacific Ocean beach or skiing on Mount Hood (even in the middle of summer, when there is lift-accessed snow skiing at one ski area). A drive through the Columbia River Gorge, a National Scenic Area, is an absolute must; and if wine is your interest, you can spend a day visiting wineries and driving through the rolling farmland that enticed pioneers to travel the Oregon Trail beginning in the 1840s.

1 The Columbia Gorge & Mount Hood Loop

If you have time for only one excursion from Portland, I strongly urge you to do the Mount Hood Loop. This is a long trip, so start your day as early as possible.

To begin your trip, take I-84 east out of Portland. At Troutdale, take the exit marked **Historic Columbia River Highway** (U.S. 30) 𝒜𝒜. This scenic highway was built between 1913 and 1922. The highway was an engineering marvel in its day, but it is dwarfed by the spectacular vistas that present themselves whenever the scenic road emerges from the dark forest. To learn more about the road and how it was built, stop at the recently restored **Vista House** 𝒜𝒜 (© **503/ 695-2230;** www.vistahouse.com), 733 feet above the river on **Crown Point.** Although there are displays of historical photos here at Vista House, most visitors can't concentrate on the exhibits, preferring to gaze at the breathtaking views that stretch for 30 miles up and down the Columbia River. Vista House is open daily from 9am to 6pm.

Between Troutdale and Ainsworth State Park, 22 miles east, you'll pass numerous waterfalls, including Latourelle, Shepherds Dell, Bridal Veil, Wahkeena, Horsetail, Oneonta, and **Multnomah Falls** 𝒜𝒜𝒜. At 620 feet from lip to pool, Multnomah Falls is the tallest waterfall in Oregon and is one of the state's top tourist attractions. Expect crowds. A paved trail leads from the base of the falls to the top and connects with other unpaved trails that are usually not at all crowded.

Not far beyond Multnomah Falls, you'll come to the narrow **Oneonta Gorge** ⟨⟨. This narrow cleft in the rock has long been a popular summertime walk for the sure of foot. The gorge can usually be explored for about ½ mile upstream to a waterfall that pours into a small pool of very cold water. There is no trail here; you just hike up the creek itself, so wear shoes that can get wet.

The next stop on your tour should be **Bonneville Lock and Dam** ⟨. One of the dam's most important features, attracting thousands of visitors each year, is its fish ladder, which allows the upriver migration of salmon. Underwater windows permit visitors to see fish as they pass through the ladder. Visit the adjacent fish hatchery to see how trout, salmon, and sturgeon are raised before they are released into the river, and be sure not to miss the underwater viewing window at the sturgeon pond. June and September are the best months to observe salmon at the fish ladder.

This is the first of many dams on the Columbia River and, along with the other dams, has been the focus of a heated environmental debate over saving the region's dwindling native wild salmon populations. Despite fish ladders and fish hatcheries, wild salmon have been fighting an upstream battle for survival. Adult salmon heading upstream to spawn have to contend with fishermen (both commercial and sport) and spawning beds that are sometimes destroyed or silted up, often by the common practice of clear-cutting timber from steep mountainsides. Among the perils faced by young salmon heading downstream are slow, warm waters that delay the journey to the Pacific Ocean, electrical turbines in dams (these kill countless numbers of fish), and irrigation culverts that often lead salmon out into farm fields. With many populations now listed as threatened species (one step below endangered species), a plan for salmon survival is being hammered out. It is hoped that the dams that once brought prosperity and cheap electricity to the Northwest won't bring about the demise of the salmon.

Not far past the dam is the **Bridge of the Gods,** a two-lane toll bridge that connects Oregon to Washington at the site where an Indian legend says a natural bridge once stood. Geologists are now convinced that this legend has its basis in a relatively recent geological event—a massive landslide that may have occurred as recently as 250 years ago. The slide completely blocked the river, and when

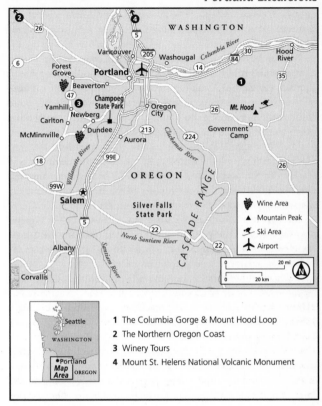

1 The Columbia Gorge & Mount Hood Loop
2 The Northern Oregon Coast
3 Winery Tours
4 Mount St. Helens National Volcanic Monument

the Columbia finally poured over the top of this natural dam, the water unleashed a 100-foot flood downstream and rapidly eroded the natural earthen dam, leaving only huge slabs of rocks in the riverbed. These rocks created the cascades for which both the Cascade Range and Cascade Locks were named.

On the Washington side of the Columbia River, east of the Bridge of the Gods, is the **Columbia Gorge Interpretive Center** *@@*, 990 SW Rock Creek Dr., Stevenson (© **800/991-2338** or 509/427-8211; www.columbiagorge.org). This modern museum is the single best introduction to the natural and human history of the Columbia Gorge and has a superb view (when it's not cloudy). Exhibits focus on the gorge's early Native American inhabitants and the development of the area by white settlers. A relic here that you can't miss is a 37-foot-high replica of a 19th-century fish wheel, which helps show how salmon runs were decimated in the past. Admission is $6 for adults, $5 for seniors and students, $4 for children 6 to 12, and free for children under 6. The center is open daily from 10am to 5pm.

Just beyond Bridge of the Gods on the Oregon side is the town of **Cascade Locks,** where you can see the navigational locks that were built to enable river traffic to avoid the treacherous passage through the cascades that once existed at this spot. In early years, many boats were portaged around the cascades instead of attempting the dangerous trip. When the locks were opened in 1896, they made traveling between The Dalles and Portland much easier. But the completion of the Historic Columbia River Highway in 1922 made the trip even easier by land. With the construction of the Bonneville Dam, the cascades were flooded, and the locks became superfluous.

The **Port of Cascade Locks Visitors Center,** which has displays on river travel in the past, is also the ticket office for the **Sternwheeler** *Columbia Gorge* ☙☙ (© **800/643-1354** or 541/374-8427; www.sternwheeler.com), which makes regular trips on the river. These cruises provide a great perspective on the Gorge. Fares for the 2-hour scenic cruises are $20 for adults, $15 for seniors, and $10 for children; dinner, lunch, breakfast, and brunch cruises run $35 to $65 for adults and $20 to $45 for children. These cruises should not be missed on a visit to the Columbia Gorge.

Anyone who windsurfs has likely heard of the town of **Hood River** ☙☙. The section of the Columbia River near this town is one of the most popular windsurfing spots in the world because of the strong winds that blow through the gorge in summer. Almost every other car in this once-sleepy little town seems to have a sailboard on the roof. If you want to try this sport yourself, stop by one of the many sailboard shops downtown for information on rentals and lessons.

If you are staying overnight on the loop, you might want to consider getting out of your car and riding the rails. The **Mount Hood Railroad** ☙, 110 Railroad Ave., Hood River (© **800/872-4661** or 541/386-3556; www.mthoodrr.com), operates an excursion train from late March to late December carrying passengers up the Hood River Valley from the town of Hood River to Parkdale and back. The railroad cars are vintage Pullman coaches, and the Mount Hood Railroad Depot is a National Historic Site. The excursions last 4 hours, and fares are $23 for adults, $21 for seniors, and $15 for children 2 to 12. The schedule varies with the season (July–Aug, the train runs Tues–Sun), so call ahead to make a reservation. There

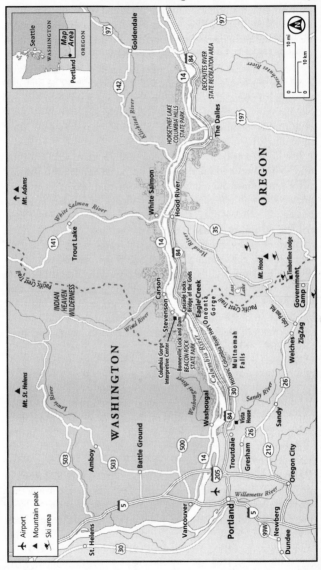

are also regularly scheduled dinner, brunch, and other specialty excursions. Mid-April's Fruit Blossom Express runs when the fruit orchards are in bloom, and in mid-October there are Harvest Festival excursions.

From Hood River, turn south on Oregon 35, passing through thousands of acres of apple and pear orchards. Every fall, roadside stands in this area sell fresh fruit and fruit products. The orchards are especially beautiful in the spring, when the trees are in bloom. No matter what time of year, you will have the snow-covered peak of Mount Hood in view as you drive through the orchards, making them all the more spectacular.

Just after Oregon 35 merges into U.S. 26, turn right onto the road to **Timberline Lodge** ⟨R⟨R . As the name implies, this lodge is at the timberline, and a July or August walk on one of the trails in the vicinity will lead you through wildflower-filled meadows. Surprisingly, because of the glacier and snowfields above the lodge, you can also ski and snowboard here all summer long.

Between Government Camp and the community of Zig Zag, watch for the roadside marker that marks the western end of the **Barlow Trail** toll road, a section of the Oregon Trail that circled around Mount Hood in order to avoid the dangerous downriver journey through the cascades of the Columbia River. There is a reproduction of the gate that once stood on this spot, and you can still see the trail itself, which is now open only to hikers, mountain bikers, and horseback riders.

To return to Portland, follow the signs for I-84 or just stay on U.S. 26 all the way back to town.

WHERE TO STAY

Bonneville Hot Springs Resort ⟨R⟨R   Although this hot springs resort doesn't have any views to speak of, it is still one of your best bets for a memorable stay in the Columbia Gorge. With lots of stone and wood detail work used in the construction, this hideaway in the woods has the feel of a modern mountain lodge, although the furnishings are more classically European in styling. The focal point of the lobby is a huge river-rock fireplace. There's an 80-foot-long mineral-water indoor pool, a full-service spa, and a big outdoor hot tub in a courtyard with an unusual stone wall down which water cascades. Guest rooms have balconies (ask for one overlooking the courtyard), beds with ornate wood headboards, and attractive bathrooms. Some of the rooms have their own mineral-water soaking tubs.

1252 E. Cascade Dr. (P.O. Box 356), North Bonneville, WA 98639. © **866/459-1678** or 509/427-7767. Fax 509/427-7733. www.bonnevilleresort.com. 78 units.

$135–$265 double; $325–$399 suite. Children under 4 stay free in parent's room. AE, DC, DISC, MC, V. **Amenities:** Restaurant (Continental); lounge; indoor pool; exercise room; full-service spa; 3 Jacuzzis; room service; massage. *In room:* A/C, TV, dataport, fridge, coffeemaker, hair dryer, iron.

Columbia Gorge Hotel ☞☞

Just west of Hood River off I-84 and in business since shortly after 1921, this little oasis of luxury offers a genteel atmosphere that was once enjoyed by Rudolph Valentino and Clark Gable. With its yellow-stucco walls and red-tile roofs, this hotel would be at home in Beverly Hills, and the hotel gardens could hold their own in Victoria, British Columbia. The hotel is perched more than 200 feet above the river on a steep cliff, and it is difficult to take your eyes off the view. At press time, the hotel was scheduled to undergo extensive renovations, so by the time you plan to visit, this historic hotel should once again be the finest hotel in the area. Be forewarned, though, that the rooms are rather cramped, as are the bathrooms. In addition to the hotel's famous breakfast, there is a complimentary champagne-and-caviar social hour each evening. On Sundays high tea is served.

4000 Westcliff Dr., Hood River, OR 97031. ⓒ **800/345-1921** or 541/386-5566. Fax 541/386-9141. www.columbiagorgehotel.com. 40 units. $199–$259 double; $279–$379 suite. Rates include multicourse breakfast. AE, DC, DISC, MC, V. Pets accepted ($25). **Amenities:** Restaurant (Northwest/Continental); lounge; concierge; business center; room service; massage and spa treatments. *In room:* A/C, TV, dataport, minibar, hair dryer, iron, free local calls, high-speed Internet access, Wi-Fi.

Skamania Lodge ☞☞☞

Boasting the most spectacular vistas of any hotel in the gorge, Skamania Lodge is also the only golf resort around. However, it is also well situated whether you brought your sailboard, hiking boots, or mountain bike. The decor is classically rustic with lots of rock and natural wood, and throughout the hotel there are Northwest Indian artworks and artifacts on display. Huge windows in the lobby have superb views of the gorge. Of course, the river-view guest rooms are more expensive than the forest-view rooms (which overlook more parking lot than forest), but these rooms are well worth the extra cost. There are also rooms with fireplaces available.

1131 Skamania Lodge Way, Stevenson, WA 98648. ⓒ **800/221-7117** or 509/427-7700. Fax 509/427-2547. www.skamania.com. 254 units. $119–$279 double; $229–$279 suite. Children under 17 stay free in parent's room. AE, DC, DISC, MC, V. **Amenities:** Restaurant (Northwest); lounge; indoor pool; 18-hole golf course; 2 tennis courts; exercise room; full-service spa; Jacuzzi; sauna; bike rentals; children's programs; activities desk; business center; room service; massage; babysitting; laundry service. *In room:* A/C, TV, dataport, minibar, coffeemaker, hair dryer, iron.

Timberline Lodge 🏮🏮   Constructed during the Great Depression of the 1930s as a WPA project, this classic alpine ski lodge overflows with craftsmanship. The grand stone fireplace, huge exposed beams, and wide plank floors of the lobby impress every first-time visitor. Woodcarvings, imaginative wrought-iron fixtures, hand-hooked rugs, and handmade furniture complete the rustic picture. Unfortunately, guest rooms, which vary considerably in size, are not as impressive as the public areas of the lodge. The smallest rooms lack private bathrooms, and windows in most rooms fail to take advantage of the phenomenal views that could be had here. However, you can always visit the Ram's Head lounge for a better view of Mount Hood.

Timberline, OR 97028. (℄ **800/547-1406** or 503/622-7979. Fax 503/622-0710. www.timberlinelodge.com. 70 units (10 without bathroom). $85–$95 double with shared bathroom; $135–$250 double with private bathroom. Children 12 and under stay free in parent's room. AE, DC, DISC, MC, V. **Amenities:** 2 restaurants (Northwest, American); 2 lounges; small outdoor pool; Jacuzzi; sauna; children's ski programs; coin-op laundry. *In room:* Dataport, hair dryer, iron, Wi-Fi.

2 The Northern Oregon Coast

One of the most beautiful coastlines in the United States, the spectacular Oregon coast is this state's main tourist destination, and it offers countless summer vacation spots along its length. The closest beaches are less than 2 hours away from Portland and offer everything from rugged coves to long sandy beaches, artists' communities to classic family beach towns.

CANNON BEACH TO NEHALEM BAY

The quickest route from Portland to the Oregon coast (80 miles) is via U.S. 26, also called the **Sunset Highway.** Just before reaching the coast and the junction with U.S. 101, watch for a sign for the **world's largest Sitka spruce tree.** This giant, more than 750 years old, is located in a small park just off the highway. Trees of this size were once common throughout the Coast Range, but almost all have now been cut down. The fight to preserve the remaining big trees is a bitter one that has divided the citizens of Oregon.

If you've got kids with you, turn north at the junction with U.S. 101 and head into **Seaside,** the coast's most traditional beach town (beachside promenade, saltwater taffy, arcade games, the works).

Otherwise, head south and watch for the turnoff to **Cannon Beach** 🏮🏮🏮 , the artsiest little town on the Oregon coast. Cannon

The Northern Oregon Coast

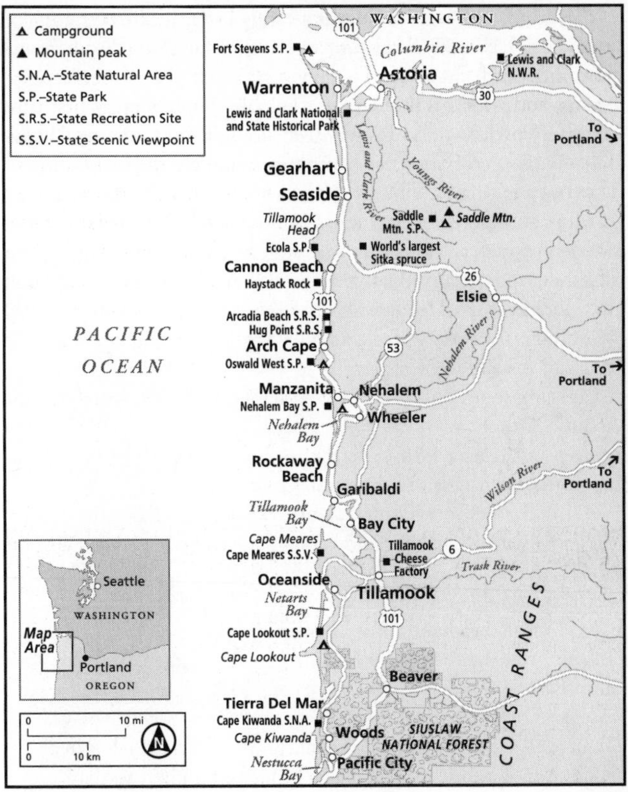
Campground
Mountain peak
S.N.A.–State Natural Area
S.P.–State Park
S.R.S.–State Recreation Site
S.S.V.–State Scenic Viewpoint
WASHINGTON
101
Fort Stevens S.P.
Columbia River
Lewis and Clark N.W.R.
Astoria
Warrenton
30
Lewis and Clark National and State Historical Park
To Portland
Lewis and Clark River
Youngs River
Gearhart
Seaside
Tillamook Head
Saddle Mtn. S.P.
Saddle Mtn.
Ecola S.P.
World's largest Sitka spruce
Cannon Beach
Haystack Rock
26
Elsie
Arcadia Beach S.R.S.
Hug Point S.R.S.
PACIFIC OCEAN
Arch Cape
53
Oswald West S.P.
Nehalem River
To Portland
Manzanita
Nehalem
Nehalem Bay S.P.
Wheeler
Nehalem Bay
Rockaway Beach
Wilson River
To Portland
Garibaldi
Tillamook Bay
Bay City
Cape Meares
Cape Meares S.S.V.
Tillamook Cheese Factory
6
Trask River
Seattle
WASHINGTON
Map Area
Portland
OREGON
Oceanside
Tillamook
Netarts Bay
101
COAST RANGES
Cape Lookout S.P.
Cape Lookout
Beaver
Tierra Del Mar
Cape Kiwanda S.N.A.
Woods
SIUSLAW NATIONAL FOREST
Cape Kiwanda
Nestucca Bay
Pacific City
0 10 mi
0 10 km
N

Beach, though quite touristy, still has so much charm, you'll likely start scheming a way to retire here yourself.

Located just north of the town of Cannon Beach is **Ecola Beach State Park** ★★ (✆ **800/551-6949** or 503/436-2844; www.oregonstateparks.org), which provides some of the most spectacular views on the coast. Here in the park there are stands of old-growth spruce, hemlock, and Douglas fir, and several trails offer a chance to walk through this lush forest. The park's Indian Beach is popular with surfers. For great views to the south, head to the Ecola Point picnic area, which is to your left just after you enter the park. A relatively easy 3-mile round-trip hiking trail connects this picnic area with Indian Beach.

Cannon Beach was named for a cannon that washed ashore here after the USS *Shark,* a military vessel, sank in 1849. Just offshore from the south end of town is **Haystack Rock** 𝔊𝔊, a massive 235-foot-tall island that is the most photographed rock on the coast. Rising up from the sand and waves at the low-tide line, Haystack Rock is a popular destination for beachcombers and tide-pool explorers. This town is packed with art galleries and interesting shops.

Every summer in early June, Cannon Beach celebrates its **Sand Castle Festival,** a celebration that attracts numerous sand sculptors and thousands of appreciative viewers. Any time of year you'll find the winds here ideal for kite flying. However, forget about doing any swimming; the waters here, and all along the Oregon coast, are too cold and rough for swimming.

Heading south out of Cannon Beach on U.S. 101, watch for the **Arcadia Beach Wayside** 𝔊𝔊. This is one of the prettiest little beaches in the area, with haystack rocks and a headland that blocks the northwest winds in the summer months.

A little farther south, you'll come to **Hug Point State Recreation Site** 𝔊𝔊, with more headland-framed beach. Here you can also see an old stretch of the original coast highway. Although the old highway was mostly just the beach, here at Hug Point the road was blasted into a headland, thus hugging the point.

A little farther south you'll come to the rugged **Oswald West State Park** 𝔊𝔊 (𝒞 **800/551-6949** or 503/436-2844; www.oregon stateparks.org), named for the governor who promoted legislation to preserve all Oregon beaches as public property. The beach is in a cove that can be reached only by walking a few hundred yards through dense forest; once you're there, all you'll hear is the crashing of the surf. The beach is strewn with huge driftwood logs that give it a wild look. High bluffs rise up at both ends of the cove, and it is possible to hike to the top of them. There are plenty of picnic tables and a walk-in campground. This is another popular surfing spot.

U.S. 101 continues south from Oswald West State Park and climbs up over **Neahkahnie Mountain** 𝔊. Legend has it that at the base of this ocean-side mountain, the survivors of a wrecked Spanish galleon buried a fortune in gold. Keep your eyes open for elk, which frequently graze in the meadows here.

Just below this windswept mountain is the quiet beach town of **Manzanita** 𝔊𝔊. Tucked under the fir, spruce, and hemlock trees are attractive summer homes. With Neahkahnie Mountain rising to the north, a long stretch of sandy beach fronting the town, and

Nehalem Bay State Park ⚲ (✆ **800/551-6949** or 503/368-5154; www.oregonstateparks.org) to the south of town, Manzanita is one of my favorite Oregon beach towns.

WHERE TO STAY
In Cannon Beach
Stephanie Inn ⚲⚲⚲   The Stephanie Inn is the most classically romantic inn on the Oregon Coast—the perfect place for an anniversary or other special weekend away. With flower boxes beneath the windows and neatly manicured gardens by the entry, the inn is reminiscent of New England's country inns, but the beach out the back door is definitely of Pacific Northwest origin. Inside, the lobby feels warm and cozy with its river-rock fireplace, huge wood columns, and beamed ceiling. The guest rooms, all individually decorated, are equally cozy, and most have double whirlpool tubs and gas fireplaces. The higher you go in the three-story inn, the better the views and the more spacious the outdoor spaces (patios, balconies, and decks). A bounteous breakfast buffet is served each morning, and there is also a complimentary afternoon wine gathering. Creative four-course prix-fixe dinners ($44) are served in the evening (reservations are required).

2740 S. Pacific St. (P.O. Box 219), Cannon Beach, OR 97110. ✆ **800/633-3466** or 503/436-2221. www.stephanie-inn.com. 50 units. $199–$399 double; $409–$469 suite. Rates include full breakfast. Children over 12 are welcome. AE, DC, DISC, MC, V. **Amenities:** Restaurant (Northwest); access to nearby health club; courtesy shopping shuttle; room service; massage. *In room:* A/C, TV/DVD, coffeemaker, hair dryer.

The Waves/The Argonauta Inn/White Heron Lodge ⚲⚲
Variety is the name of the game in eclectic Cannon Beach, and The Waves plays the game better than any other accommodations in town. This lodge, only a block from the heart of town, consists of more than four dozen rooms, suites, cottages, and beach houses at The Waves and two other jointly managed lodges, The Argonauta Inn and the White Heron Lodge. The Garden Court rooms (with no ocean views) are the least expensive. My favorites, however, are the cottages of The Argonauta Inn. Surrounded by beautiful flower gardens in the summer, these old oceanfront cottages capture the spirit of Cannon Beach. For sybarites and romantics, there are fireplaces in some rooms and whirlpool spas overlooking the ocean. If you want to get away from the crowds, ask for an apartment at the recently renovated White Heron Lodge. The Waves itself offers contemporary accommodations, some of which are right on the beach and have great views.

188 W. 2nd St. (P.O. Box 3), Cannon Beach, OR 97110. ✆ 800/822-2468 or 503/436-2205. Fax 503/436-1490. www.thewavesmotel.com. 55 units. $84–$389 double. 3-night minimum July–Aug; 2-night minimum on weekends Sept–June. Children under 6 stay free in parent's room. DISC, MC, V. **Amenities:** Jacuzzi; massage; coin-op laundry. *In room:* TV/VCR, dataport, kitchen, fridge, coffeemaker, hair dryer, iron, free local calls.

In Manzanita

Coast Cabins *&& Finds* These five modern cabins are set back a ways from the beach but are the most impressive cabins on the entire coast. Done in a sort of modern interpretation of Scandinavian cabins, these accommodations are designed as romantic getaways for couples. Two of the cabins are tall, two-story structures, and the second-floor bedrooms have walls of windows. The cabin interiors are well designed and artfully decorated, with such touches as Tibetan carpets, original art, and unusual lighting fixtures. Now imagine the burnished glow of the cabins' cedar exteriors accented by lovely terraced perennial gardens, and you'll have an idea of just how the perfect getaway on the Oregon coast should look.

635 Laneda Ave., Manzanita, OR 97130. ✆ 503/368-7113. www.coastcabins.com. 5 units. $110–$295 double. 2-night minimum on weekends and throughout the summer. AE, MC, V. Pets accepted ($25). *In room:* TV/VCR, kitchen, fridge, coffeemaker, hair dryer, iron, free local calls, Wi-Fi.

WHERE TO DINE
In Cannon Beach

Bistro Restaurant *&&* NORTHWEST If you're looking for atmosphere and good food, this is the place. Bistro Restaurant is set back a bit from the street behind a small garden and down a brick walkway. Step through the door, and you'll think you've just walked into a French country inn. Stucco walls, old prints of flowers, and fresh flowers on the tables are the only decor this tiny place can afford without growing cramped. Dining choices here include exquisitely prepared seafood dishes such as pan-fried oysters, crab cakes, and seafood stew. There's live music on weekend evenings, and even a tiny bar.

263 N. Hemlock St. ✆ 503/436-2661. Reservations highly recommended. Main courses $14–$24. MC, V. Daily 5–9:30pm or 10pm; closed Tues–Wed in off season.

Gower Street Bistro *&&* NEW AMERICAN This little restaurant is positively adorable. The white tile floors, wicker chairs, white wainscoting, pressed-tin ceiling, and display case full of imported meats and cheese all set the scene for superb food. The quiches (served at breakfast, lunch, and dinner) are big, fat works of art that should not be missed, although I can never pass up the pulled-pork sandwich, which is the best I've had outside of North Carolina. At dinner, start with a charcuterie or cheese plate and then go for the 40-clove chicken with calvados or the down-home meatloaf.

1116 S. Hemlock St. ⓒ 503/436-2729. www.gowerstreetbistro.com. Reservations recommended. Main courses $9–$13 lunch, $10–$30 dinner. AE, DISC, MC, V. Summer daily 8am–10pm; other months daily 9am–9pm.

In Nehalem

Currents ⑨ NORTHWEST   The creative food here alone would make this one of my favorite north-coast restaurants, but in addition to having great food, Currents has a wonderfully relaxing deck overlooking the Nehalem River just a couple of miles from picturesque Manzanita. From start to finish, offerings here are exceedingly complex, with flavors running rampant on your taste buds. Start with shrimp-and-squash bisque with truffle crème fraîche, smoked rockfish, and crispy prosciutto, or perhaps Moroccan crab cakes. Next, I recommend the braised beef short ribs with truffle-fig tapenade or the grilled rockfish with a crab, fennel, and marscapone crepe. Think sunset dinner, and you'll have an unforgettable meal. Currents is also a fun destination to paddle to if you rented a kayak in nearby Wheeler.

35815 U.S. 101, Nehalem. ⓒ 503/368-5557. Main courses $6–$8 lunch, $15–$23 dinner. MC, V. Wed–Sun noon–3pm and 6–9pm.

TILLAMOOK & THE THREE CAPES SCENIC LOOP

The other dramatic stretch of beach close to Portland is west of the dairy-farming town of Tillamook and is called the **Three Capes Scenic Loop** ⑨⑨. To reach this rugged stretch of the Oregon coast, head west from Portland on U.S. 26 (Sunset Hwy.), and, about 25 miles west of Portland near the town of Banks, take Oregon 6 toward Tillamook. Allow about 2 hours to get to Tillamook from Portland.

Two miles north of **Tillamook** on U.S. 101, you can visit the **Tillamook Cheese Factory** ⑨ (ⓒ 800/542-7290 or 503/815-1300; www.tillamookcheese.com). The Tillamook area is one of Oregon's main dairy-farming locations, and much of the milk is turned into cheddar cheese and butter. Today the cheese factory is one of the most popular attractions on the Oregon coast. You can watch the cheese-making process through large windows, buy an ice-cream cone, and pick up an assortment of tasty cheeses for a picnic.

Just west of Tillamook is the start of the Three Capes Scenic Route, which leads to Cape Meares, Cape Lookout, and Cape Kiwanda, all of which provide stunning vistas of rocky cliffs, misty mountains, and booming surf. As the name implies, this is a very scenic stretch of road, and there are plenty of places to stop and enjoy the views and the beaches.

Cape Meares State Scenic Viewpoint ✺ perches high atop the cape, with the Cape Meares lighthouse just a short walk from the parking lot. This lighthouse, 200 feet above the water, was built in 1890. Today it has been replaced by an automated light a few feet away. Be sure to visit the **octopus tree** here in the park. This Sitka spruce has been twisted and sculpted by harsh weather.

As you come down from the cape, you'll reach the village of **Oceanside** ✺, which clings to the steep mountainsides of a small cove. One tavern, one restaurant, and one cafe are the only commercial establishments, and that's the way folks here like it. If you walk north along the beach, you'll find a pedestrian tunnel through the headland that protects this hillside community. Through the tunnel is another beautiful stretch of beach.

South of Oceanside, the road runs along a flat stretch of beach before reaching **Cape Lookout State Park** ✺✺ (© **800/551-6949** or 503/842-4981; www.oregonstateparks.org). Cape Lookout, a steep forested ridge jutting out into the Pacific, is an excellent place for whale-watching in the spring. A trail leads out to the end of the point from either the main (lower) parking area or the parking area at the top of the ridge. From the upper parking lot, it is a 5-mile round-trip hike to the end of the point.

South of Cape Lookout you come to **Pacific City** and **Cape Kiwanda** ✺✺, the last of the three capes on this scenic loop. Cape Kiwanda, a state natural area, is a sandstone headland backed by a huge sand dune that is popular with hang gliders. It's also fun to climb to the top and then run down. From the top of this giant dune, it is sometimes possible to spot spouting gray whales. Just offshore is another **Haystack Rock** ✺✺, every bit as picturesque as the one in Cannon Beach. Because this huge rock breaks the waves, the beach here is used by beach-launched dories, as well as surfers. The Pelican Pub & Brewery right on the beach here makes a good spot for dinner before heading back to Portland.

To return to Portland from Pacific City, follow signs to U.S. 101 and head north to **Tillamook.** From there, just retrace your outbound route by taking Oregon 6 back to U.S. 26.

WHERE TO STAY

Inn at Cape Kiwanda ✺✺ *Finds* Although it's across the street from the beach (and Cape Kiwanda State Natural Area), this modern cedar-shingled three-story hotel has one of the best views on the Oregon coast: Directly offshore rises Haystack Rock, a huge jug-handled monolith. Since a great view isn't quite enough, the hotel was designed with luxurious, contemporary rooms, all of which have balconies and fireplaces. A few have whirlpool tubs, and there is also a very luxurious suite. The corner rooms are my favorites. The inn is affiliated with the Pelican Pub & Brewery, which is right across the street, and on the inn's ground floor there is an art gallery, a salon with massage services, and an espresso bar that also sells wine and books.

33105 Cape Kiwanda Dr., Pacific City, OR 97135. ☏ 888/965-7001 or 503/965-7001. Fax 503/965-7002. www.innatcapekiwanda.com. 35 units. $109–$249 double; $199–$309 suite. 2-night minimum on holidays and weekends in July–Aug. Children under 18 stay free in parent's room. AE, DISC, MC, V. Pets accepted ($20). **Amenities:** Restaurant (brewpub); lounge; exercise room; bike rentals; business center; room service; massage; coin-op laundry. *In room:* TV/DVD, fridge, coffeemaker, hair dryer, free local calls, Wi-Fi.

WHERE TO DINE

Pelican Pub & Brewery ☙ PUB FOOD With massive Haystack Rock looming just offshore and the huge dune of Cape Kiwanda just up the beach, this brewpub claims the best view of any pub in Oregon. The Pelican is right on the beach and even has its own beach volleyball court. There's a good selection of brews, including Tsunami Stout and my personal favorite, the Doryman's Dark Ale. Sandwiches, burgers, fabulous fish and chips, and pizzas are the menu mainstays here. The steamed clams served with barley bread made from beer grain are divine. Kids are welcome, and the beach location makes this a great spot for lunch or dinner if you're hanging out on the beach all day.

33180 Cape Kiwanda Dr. ☏ 503/965-7007. www.pelicanbrewery.com. Main courses $9–$20. AE, DISC, MC, V. Sun–Thurs 8am–9pm; Fri–Sat 8am–10pm (closes 1 hr. later in summer).

3 Winery Tours

For several decades now, Oregon wines, particularly pinot noirs, have been winning awards. This isn't surprising when you consider that Oregon is on the same latitude as the wine-growing regions of France. The climate is also very similar—cool, wet winters and springs and long, dry summers with warm days and cool nights. These are ideal conditions for growing wine grapes, and local vineyards are making the most of a good situation.

A free Oregon winery guide describing around 100 Oregon wineries is available from the **Oregon Wine Center,** 1200 NW

Naito Pkwy., Suite 400, Portland, OR 97209 (© **503/228-8336;** www.oregonwine.org), or at the **Portland Oregon Visitors Association Information Center,** 701 SW Sixth Ave., Portland, OR 97205 (© **877/678-5263** or 503/275-8355; www.travelportland.com).

There are more than 50 wineries within an hour's drive of Portland, and you could easily spend a week getting to know them. However, for an afternoon of wine tasting, I suggest visiting only three or four wineries. A trip through wine country is a chance not only to sample a wide range of wines, but also to see the fertile valleys that lured pioneers across the Oregon Trail. I recommend taking along a picnic lunch, which you can, of course, supplement with a wine purchase. Most wineries have picnic tables, and many of them have lovely views. During the summer many wineries stage weekend festivals that include live music.

The easiest way to visit the Oregon wine country is to head southwest out of Portland on Oregon 99 West. Between the towns of Newberg and Dundee, you'll find more than half a dozen wineries right alongside the highway and an equal number tucked into the hills within a few miles of the highway. Along Oregon 99 West, wineries are well marked by official highway-department signs. The first winery I recommend stopping at is the small, new **August Cellars,** 14000 NE Quarry Rd., Newberg (© **503/554-6766;** www. augustcellars.com), which is located just east of Newberg. Just downhill from this winery is **Rex Hill Vineyards,** 30835 N. Ore. 99W, Newberg (© **800/739-4455;** www.rexhill.com), one of Oregon's largest and most reliable wineries. The next along the highway are in Dundee. My favorites here include the **Pinot Station Tasting Room,** 240 SE Fifth St., Dundee (© **503/538-7100;** www.dobbes familyestate.com); the **Ponzi Wine Bar,** 100 SW Seventh St., Dundee (© **503/554-1500;** www.ponziwinebar.com); **Argyle Winery,** 691 Ore. 99W, Dundee (© **888/4-ARGYLE** or 503/538-8520; www.argylewinery.com); and **Sokol Blosser,** 5000 Sokol Blosser Lane, Dundee (© **800/582-6668** or 503/864-2282; www. sokolblosser.com).

Continue a little past Dundee, and you can visit three of the most highly regarded wineries in the state: **Archery Summit,** 18599 NE Archery Summit Rd., Dayton (© **800/732-8822;** www.archery summit.com); **Domaine Drouhin Oregon,** Breyman Orchards Road, Dayton (© **503/864-2700;** www.domainedrouhin.com); and **Domaine Serene,** 6555 Hilltop Lane, Dayton (© **866/864-6555** or 503/864-4600; www.domaineserene.com). All three of these wineries specialize in producing world-class pinot noir.

In the town of Carlton, 7 miles north of McMinnville on Oregon 47, you'll find a concentration of good wineries. At **The Tasting Room,** 105 W. Main St. (℃ **503/852-6733;** www.pinotnoir.com), you can taste wines from wineries that are not usually open to the public. Most wines featured here are from wineries in the immediate vicinity of Carlton. Also here in Carlton, you'll find the **Carlton Winemakers Studio,** 801 N. Scott St. (℃ **503/852-6100;** www. winemakersstudio.com), which represents numerous wineries, including Andrew Rich Wines, Hamacher Wines, and Domaine Meriwether. Adjacent to this latter winery, you'll find **Cuneo Cellars,** 750 Lincoln St. (℃ **503/852-0002;** www.cuneocellars.com), which is known for its big, full-bodied red wines. A few blocks away, you can stop in at **Tyrus Evan/The Depot,** 120 N. Pine St. (℃ **503/852-7010;** www.thecarltondepot.com), which specializes in bordeaux and Rhone varietals. Outside the town of Yamhill, don't miss the impressive **Willakenzie Estate,** 19143 NE Laughlin Rd., Yamhill (℃ **888/953-9463** or 503/662-3280; www.willakenzie. com), or **Penner-Ash Wine Cellars,** 15771 NE Ribbon Ridge Rd. (℃ **503/554-5545;** www.pennerash.com). Nearby you'll also find the economical **Laurel Ridge Winery,** 13301 NE Kuehne Rd., Carlton (℃ **503/852-7050**).

WHERE TO STAY

Black Walnut Inn 𝒜𝒜 Perched high in the Red Hills of Dundee with a view that seems to take in all of Oregon wine country, this inn looks for all the world as though it had been transported here from Tuscany. Although guest rooms don't have the same Tuscan feel, they are comfortably homey. Some have antique furnishings and some are more contemporary, so there's a room that's just right for nearly anyone. Some rooms have a soaking tub, and all have a balcony or patio. The gardens and patios here are the perfect place to sip a glass of wine at sunset.

9600 NE Worden Hill Rd., Dundee, OR 97115. ℃ **866/429-4114** or 503/429-4114. Fax 503/538-4194. www.blackwalnut-inn.com. 7 units. $180–$575 suite. Rates include full breakfast. AE, MC, V. Children 12 and older accepted. **Amenities:** Concierge; massage. *In room:* A/C, TV/DVD/VCR, hair dryer, free local calls, high-speed Internet access.

McMenamins Hotel Oregon 𝒜 This restored historic hotel in downtown McMinnville is operated by a Portland-based chain of brewpubs, nightclubs, and unusual hotels that are all filled with interesting artwork. Guest rooms here are done in a simple, classic style, with antique and reproduction furniture. The corner kings with private bathrooms and big windows on two sides are the nicest rooms; however, most rooms here have shared bathrooms. Offsetting this inconvenience is the hotel's genuinely historic feel. The ground-floor brewpub/dining room, cellar bar, and rooftop bar and deck overlooking McMinnville and the Yamhill Valley all help make the Hotel Oregon imminently recommendable. There are also a couple of good restaurants within a few blocks.

310 NE Evans St., McMinnville, OR 97128. ⓒ 888/472-8427 or 503/472-8427. www.mcmenamins.com. 42 units (6 with private bathroom). $50–$95 double with shared bathroom; $80–$110 double with private bathroom. Rates include full breakfast. Children 6 and under stay free in parent's room. AE, DC, DISC, MC, V. **Amenities:** Restaurant (American); 3 lounges. *In room:* A/C.

Springbrook Hazelnut Farm ⓇⓇ Located only 20 miles from Portland, this 70-acre working farm is a convenient rural getaway for anyone who craves a slower-paced vacation. The four craftsman-style buildings are listed on the National Register of Historic Places and include the main house, a carriage house, and a cottage. Original artwork abounds in the boldly decorated, colorful main house. Both of the main buildings overlook the farm's pond and lovely back garden, and there are also tennis courts and a swimming pool. Through the hazelnut orchard is Rex Hill Vineyards, and there's also a small winery operating here on the farm. The little white cottage, with its antique fireplace mantle, fir floors, and tiled bathroom, overlooks the farm's pond and a meadow that's filled with daffodils in the spring.

30295 N. Ore. 99W, Newberg, OR 97132. ⓒ 800/793-8528 or 503/538-4606. www.nutfarm.com. 2 units. $225 cottage or carriage house. Rates include full breakfast. AE, DC, DISC, MC, V. **Amenities:** Outdoor pool; tennis court. *In room:* Kitchen, fridge, coffeemaker, hair dryer, iron, no phone.

Youngberg Hill Inn ⓇⓇ Set on a 50-acre farm that includes pinot noir vineyards, this is the quintessential wine-country inn. A mile-long gravel driveway leads to the inn, which sits atop a hill with commanding views of the Willamette Valley, snow-capped Cascades peaks, and the Coast Range. Large decks wrap around both floors of the inn, and some of the rooms have their own fireplaces. Big breakfasts get visitors off to a good start each morning. Pull up a chair on the porch, pour a glass of the inn's own pinot noir, gaze out over the rolling hills, and you'll probably start thinking about cashing in the mutual funds to start a vineyard of your own.

10660 SW Youngberg Hill Rd., McMinnville, OR 97128. ⓒ 888/657-8668 or 503/ 472-2727. Fax 503/472-1313. www.youngberghill.com. 7 units. $149–$179 double;

$199–$249 suite. Rates include full breakfast. MC, V. Children over 4 are welcome. **Amenities:** Massage. *In room:* A/C, hair dryer, iron, free local calls, Wi-Fi.

WHERE TO DINE

Bistro Maison ⑂ FRENCH   This cozy little spot in an old house in downtown McMinnville is a casual French restaurant with great food. The husband-and-wife owners bring loads of experience to the restaurant, including time spent at famed New York restaurants *The Russian Tea Room* and *Tavern on the Green.* The menu offers such French standards as escargot and coq au vin, but whatever you order for an entree, be sure to start with the mussels or the very authentic fondue. There are daily plats du jour, with Sundays featuring a good cassoulet. Although the service here can be hit-or-miss, the food is good enough to overlook most shortcomings on the part of the waitstaff. In summer, ask for a table on the tree-shaded patio.

729 NE 3rd St. ② 503/474-1888. www.bistromaison.com. Reservations recommended. Main courses $9–$12 lunch, $16–$18 dinner. DISC, MC, V. Wed–Thurs 11:30am–2pm and 5–8pm; Fri 11:30am–2pm and 5–9pm; Sat 5–9pm; Sun noon–8pm.

Cuvée ⑂⑂ FRENCH   Chef/owner Gilbert Henry had long established himself as one of the top toques in Portland before moving recently to the small town of Carlton in the heart of the wine country. Here Henry's classic French cuisine is the perfect foil for fine wines from Carlton-area wineries. The boeuf bourguignon is the perfect dish to go with a local pinot, but there's also usually a lamb dish (perhaps cassoulet or lamb chops) on the menu. Be sure to start your meal with some oysters or sautéed mushrooms and local pinot gris or chardonnay. Attached to the restaurant is a cute little shop—**Lulu** (② **503/852-6777**)—that sells hand-picked imports from France.

214 W. Main St., Carlton. ② 503/852-6555. Reservations highly recommended. Main courses $18–$23. AE, DISC, MC, V. Wed–Sat 5:30–9:30pm; Sun 4–8pm.

The Dundee Bistro ⑂⑂ NORTHWEST   Located in the same building as the Ponzi Wine Bar and the Your Northwest gift shop, this chic eatery would be right at home in Portland's trendy Pearl District. The bistro's hip, urban style, however, also sums up a modern wine-country aesthetic, which makes this place quite popular with people touring the area wineries. The menu is relatively short and changes on a regular basis to reflect seasonal ingredients. However, the emphasis is on fresh regional ingredients, which translates into the likes of smoked salmon carpaccio with orange, olive tapenade, capers, and shaved fennel; and pork loin with Parmesan polenta and chanterelle mushrooms; beef shoulder with cannelloni beans and spinach and truffled foie gras butter. The wine list focuses on area wines.

100-A SW 7th St., Dundee. ✆ 503/554-1650. www.dundeebistro.com. Reservations recommended. Main courses $12–$24. AE, MC, V. Sun–Thurs 11:30am–8:30pm; Fri–Sat 11:30am–9pm.

The Joel Palmer House 🐿🐿🐿 FRENCH/NORTHWEST If you love mushrooms in all their earthy guises, then in this downtown Dayton restaurant you will find your culinary Nirvana. Chef/owner Jack Czarnecki is a man obsessed with mushrooms, and nearly every dish has mushrooms in it. Start your meal with the extraordinary wild mushroom soup made with suillis mushrooms, then move on to the filet mignon with pinot noir sauce and wild mushrooms or the beef Stroganoff with Oregon white truffles. The rack of lamb with a pinot-hazelnut sauce, although it lacks mushrooms, is a quintessential-wine country entree. The extensive wine list features Oregon wines. The restaurant is in a house built in the 1850s and is quite formal. Mushroom lovers will be in good hands if they opt for the "Jack's Mushroom Madness" prix-fixe dinner.

600 Ferry St., Dayton. ✆ 503/864-2995. www.joelpalmerhouse.com. Reservations highly recommended. Main courses $18–$28; prix fixe $55. AE, DC, DISC, MC, V. Tues–Sat 5–9pm; closed mid-Feb to mid-Mar.

Tina's 🐿🐿 CONTINENTAL/NORTHWEST Despite its rather small and nondescript building right on the highway in Dundee, Tina's has long been one of the Yamhill County wine country's premier restaurants, and with its contemporary menu and decor, it's my favorite place to eat in the area. The menu changes regularly and usually has no more than half a dozen entrees and fewer appetizers. However, a balance between the traditional (grilled rib-eye steak with portobello mushrooms and hand-cut fries) and the less familiar (pan-roasted duck breast with corn soufflé and green-peppercorn sauce) keeps diners content. There are usually almost as many desserts available as there are entrees, and the wine selection, of course, emphasizes local wines.

760 Hwy. 99W. ✆ 503/538-8880. www.tinasdundee.com. Reservations recommended. Main courses $8–$10 lunch, $22–$30 dinner. AE, DISC, MC, V. Tues–Fri 11:30am–2pm and 5–9pm; Sat–Sun 5–9pm.

4 Mount St. Helens National Volcanic Monument

Named in 1792 by Capt. George Vancouver for his friend Baron St. Helens, Mount St. Helens was once considered the most perfect of

Mount St. Helens National Volcanic Monument

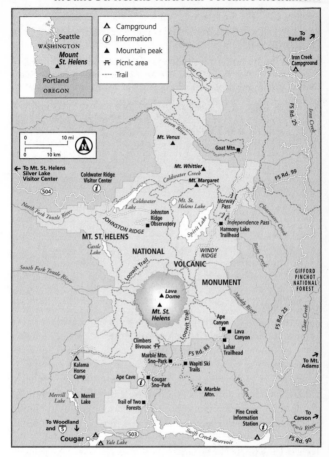

the Cascade peaks, a snow-covered cone rising above lush forests. However, on May 18, 1980, all that changed when Mount St. Helens erupted with a violent explosion previously unknown in modern times.

The eruption blew out the side of the volcano and removed the top 1,300 feet of the peak, causing the largest landslide in recorded history. This blast is estimated to have traveled at up to 650 mph, with air temperatures of up to 800°F (425°C). The eruption also sent more than 540 million tons of ash nearly 16 miles into the atmosphere. This massive volume of ash rained down on an area of 22,000 square miles and could be measured as far away as Denver.

Today the volcano and 110,000 acres of both devastated and undisturbed forests have been preserved as Mount St. Helens National Volcanic Monument. Several visitor centers provide information on the eruption and the subsequent changes that have taken place here. At press time, the volcano was once again active, with a new cone forming inside the crater. This renewed activity, though not as dramatic as the 1980 eruption, makes Mount St. Helens the only active volcano in the contiguous United States.

The monument is located roughly 90 miles north of Portland off I-5 (take the Castle Rock exit). Admission to one monument visitor center (or Ape Cave) is $3 for adults, and to two or more visitor centers (and Ape Cave) is $6. If you just want to park at one of the monument's trail heads and go for a hike, all you need is a valid Northwest Forest Pass, which costs $5 per day. If it's winter, you'll need a Sno-Park Permit ($8–$9 per day).

For more information on the national monument, contact **Mount St. Helens National Volcanic Monument,** 42218 NE Yale Bridge Rd., Amboy, WA 98601 (© **360/247-3900;** www.fs.fed.us/gpnf/mshnvm).

The best place to start an exploration of the monument is the **Mount St. Helens Silver Lake Visitor Center** (© **360/274-0962;** www.parks.wa.gov/mountsthelens.asp), which is operated by Washington State Parks and is located at Silver Lake, 5 miles east of Castle Rock on Highway 504. The visitor center houses extensive exhibits on the eruption and its effects on the region. April through October, it's open daily from 9am to 5pm in summer (until 4pm in other months). Before reaching the center, you can stop and watch a 25-minute 70mm film about the eruption at the **Mount St. Helens Cinedome Theater** (© **360/274-9844;** www.thecinedome.com), at exit 49 off I-5; tickets cost $6 for adults, $5 for seniors and children.

Continuing east from the visitor center, at milepost 27, you'll come to the **Hoffstadt Bluffs Visitor Center** (© **360/274-7750;** www.mt-st-helens.com). This is primarily just a snack bar and take-off site for 25-minute helicopter flights over Mount St. Helens ($114 with a three-person minimum), but there are also great views. From May to September this visitor center is open daily from 10am to 7pm, shorter hours in other months.

A few miles farther, just past milepost 33, is the **Charles W. Bingham Forest Learning Center** (© 360/414-3439), open mid-May through mid-October daily from 10am to 6pm (until 5pm in Oct). This is primarily a promotional center for the timber industry, but, in a theater designed to resemble an ash-covered landscape, you can watch a short, fascinating video about the eruption. If you happen to have young children with you, let them blow off steam at the great little playground here. Outside both the Hoffstadt Bluffs Visitor Center and the Forest Learning Center, you can usually see numerous elk on the floor of the Toutle River Valley far below.

The **Coldwater Ridge Visitor Center** (© 360/274-2114), at milepost 47 on Washington 504, only 8 miles from the crater, is the second of the national monument's official visitor centers. It features interpretive displays on the events leading up to the eruption and the subsequent slow regeneration of life around the volcano. You'll also find a picnic area, interpretive trail, restaurant, and boat launch at Coldwater Lake. May through October, the visitor center is open daily from 10am to 6pm (other months hours are reduced).

Of the many visitor centers, none offers a more awe-inspiring view than that from the **Johnston Ridge Observatory** (© 360/274-2140), 10 miles past the Coldwater Ridge Visitor Center. Built into the mountainside and designed to blend into the landscape, this observatory houses the equipment that is still used to monitor activity within Mount St. Helens. The observatory is open from early May to October daily from 10am to 6pm. If you're up for a bit of hiking, the single best choice on this side of the monument is the **Boundary Ridge Trail,** which heads east from the Johnston Ridge Observatory, with a jaw-dropping view of the blast zone the entire way. This trail leads for many miles across the monument, so you can hike as much or as little as you want. There is a good turn-around point about 1 mile out from the observatory.

For a different perspective on the devastation wrought by Mount St. Helens's eruption, drive around to the mountain's east side and take the road up to Windy Ridge. Although it takes a couple of hours longer to get to this side of the mountain, you will be rewarded by equally amazing views, better hiking opportunities, and smaller crowds. To reach the east side of the mountain, take U.S. 12 east from exit 68 off I-5. In Randle, head south on Forest Road 25. The **Woods Creek Information Station,** on Forest Road 25 just before the junction with Route 26, has information on this part of the monument.

South of Woods Creek, watch for Forest Road 99, the road to the Windy Ridge Viewpoint. This road crosses many miles of blown-down trees that were felled by a single blast, a reminder of the awesome power of nature. More than 25 years after the eruption, life is slowly returning to the devastated forest. At the **Windy Ridge Viewpoint,** visitors get one of the best close-up views of the crater. A staircase climbs 220 feet up the hill above the parking area for even better views. Below Windy Ridge lies Spirit Lake, once one of the most popular summer vacation spots in the Washington Cascades. Today the lake is desolate and lifeless. The 1-mile Harmony Trail leads down to the shore of Spirit Lake and is a very worthwhile hike. Just keep in mind that it is a 600-foot climb back up to the trail head parking lot.

If you're an experienced hiker in good physical condition, consider climbing to the top of Mount St. Helens. From the trail head on the south side of the mountain, the hike takes 8 to 10 hours and can require an ice ax. Climbing permits ($15) are required, and because the climb is very popular, it is advisable to make a reservation (© **360/449-7861;** www.fs.fed.us/gpnf/mshnvm). Reservations are taken beginning on February 1, and summer weekends book up fast. If you don't have a reservation, you can try your luck by stopping at **Jack's Restaurant and Store,** on Washington 503, 23 miles east of the town of Woodland. Each evening at 6pm, this store has a lottery of climbing permits for the next day. Between November 1 and March 31, permits are free and no reservation is necessary—but expect lots of snow. Currently, because of increased volcanic activity within the crater of Mount St. Helens, climbing to the crater rim is prohibited. Check with the monument before planning this climb.

The south side of the monument was the least affected by the eruption and consequently does not offer the dramatic scenes of devastation to be seen on the east and west sides of the monument. However, this area offers some good hiking and a couple of very interesting volcanic features. The first of these features you'll come to is the **Ape Cave,** a lava tube that was formed 1,900 years ago when lava poured from the volcano. When the lava finally stopped flowing, it left a 2-mile-long cave that is the longest continuous lava tube in the Western Hemisphere. At the Ape's Headquarters, you can join a regular ranger-led exploration of the cave or rent a lantern for exploring the cave on your own. This center is open daily from late June to Labor Day.

Of the trails on this side of the monument, the **Lava Canyon Trail** is the most fascinating. It follows a canyon that was unearthed by a mudflow that swept down this side of the mountain after the eruption.

Hikers will find many other hiking trails within the monument, some in blast zones and some in forests that were left undamaged by the eruption. Ask at any visitor center for trail information.

Index

See also Accommodations and Restaurants indexes below.

GENERAL INDEX

A
AAA (American Automobile Association), 33, 38
Accommodations, 41–56. *See also* Accommodations Index
  best, 3–5
  family-friendly, 51
  surfing for, 21–22
Addresses, finding, 31–32
Aequis, 98
Airfares, 20–21, 26
Airlines, 24
Airport
  accommodations near, 54–56
  arriving at, 28
  security, 25
Airport MAX (Red Line), 28
Aladdin Theater, 116
Alameda Brewhouse, 121
Alotto Gelato, 75
American Express, 11, 38
Amnesia Brewing Company, 121
Amtrak, 27, 30
Andrea's Cha-Cha Club, 115
Antiques, 104–105
Ape Cave, 148
Arcadia Beach Wayside, 134
Archery Summit (Dayton), 140
Area codes, 38
Argyle Winery (Dundee), 140
Arlene Schnitzer Concert Hall (the Schnitz), 2, 112, 114
Art galleries, 105–106
Art glass, 106
Artists Repertory Theatre, 115
Arts and crafts, 106–108
ATMs (automated-teller machines), 10–11
Augen Gallery, 105
August Cellars (Newberg), 140
Auto racing, 97
Avalon Hotel & Spa, 98
Aveda Lifestyle Store and Spa, 98

B
Babysitters, 38
Bagdad Theater, 124
Bakeries, 74
Barlow Trail, 130
Barnes & Noble, 106
Bar Pastiche, 122
Bars and pubs, 117–124
Bartini, 117
Baseball, 97–98
Basketball, 98
Bed & breakfasts (B&Bs), 44
Beer, 118–119
Berbati's Pan, 116
The Berry Botanic Garden, 89–90
Biking, 7–8, 93–94
The Bite of Oregon, 14
Blackfish Gallery, 105
The Blue Monk on Belmont, 115
Blues, 116
Blue Sky Whitewater Rafting, 97
Boat tours and cruises, 8, 91–92
Bonneville Lock and Dam, 126
Bookstores, 106
Borders, 106
Boundary Ridge Trail, 147
The Brazen Bean, 117
Brewpubs, 2, 118, 120–122
Bridge of the Gods, 126–127
Bridge Tour, 92–93
Broadway in Portland series, 115
Brunish Hall, 112
The Bullseye Connection, 106
The Bullseye Connection Gallery, 106
Bus tours, 92
Bus travel, 27, 35

C
Cafes, 73
Calendar of events, 13–15
Cannon Beach, 132–137
Cape Kiwanda, 138
Cape Lookout State Park, 138
Cape Meares State Scenic Viewpoint, 138

Carlton Winemakers Studio, 141
Car rentals, 22, 36–37
Car travel, 26–27
Cascade Locks, 128
C.C. Slaughters Nightclub & Lounge, 123
Cellphones, 23–24
Chamber Music Northwest, 114
Changes, 109
Charles W. Bingham Forest Learning Center, 147
Chinatown, 33. *See also* Downtown walking tour, 99–103
Christmas at Pittock Mansion, 15
Classical Chinese Garden, 83–84, 100
Classical music, 114
Club and music scene, 115–117
Coldwater Ridge Visitor Center, 147
The Columbia Gorge, 125–132
Columbia Gorge, Sternwheeler, 128
Columbia Gorge Interpretive Center (Stevenson), 127–128
Columbia Sportswear Company, 109
Columbia Sportswear Company Factory Outlet Store, 109
Contemporary Crafts Museum & Gallery, 106
Council Crest, 6, 86
Crafts, 106–108
Credit cards, 11
Crown Point, 125
Crush Bar, 123
Crystal Ballroom, 116
Crystal Springs Rhododendron Garden, 90
Cultural District, 33
Cuneo Cellars (Carlton), 141

Dance clubs, 115
Dance performances, 113–114
Darcelle's XV, 115
Day spas, 98
Dentists, 38
Department stores, 108
Disabilities, travelers with, 17–19
Doctors, 38
Do Jump! Extremely Physical Theatre, 113–114
Dolores Winningstad Theater, 112
Domaine Drouhin Oregon (Dayton), 140
Domaine Serene (Dayton), 140
Doug Fir Lounge, 117

Downtown (including the Skidmore Historic District & Chinatown), 33
accommodations, 44–49
brewpub, 120
restaurants, 57–63
sights and attractions, 77–84
Driving rules, 37

Eagle Bar, 123
Eastbank Esplanade, 81–82
Eastmoreland Golf Course, 94
Ecola Beach State Park, 133
Ecotrust's Jean Vollum Natural Capital Center, 102–103
Edgefield Theater, 124
Elk Rock Garden of the Bishop's Close, 90
The Embers Avenue, 124
Emergencies, 38

Families with children, 20
best activities for, 8–9
sights and attractions, 90–91
Fareless Square, 7, 31, 35
Fashions (clothing), 108–109
Festivals and special events, 13–15
Film Festival, Portland International, 13
Finnegan's Toys and Gifts, 110
First Thursday Art Walk, 7, 34, 105
Forest Park, 8, 85, 94–95
Fourth of July Fireworks (Vancouver, WA), 14
Free or almost free activities, 6–7

Gay and lesbian travelers, 19, 123–124
Gelaterias, 75
Gifts and souvenirs, 110
Golf, 94
Grape Escape, 93
Gray Line, 92
Greyhound Bus Lines, 30

Half-Price Ticket Hotline, 113
Hawthorne/Belmont District, 34
Haystack Rock, 134, 138
Health concerns, 17
Health insurance, 16
Heron Lakes Golf Course, 94

Highways, 31
Hiking, 2, 8, 94–95
Historic Columbia River Highway (U.S. 30), 125
Hoffman Gallery, 106–107
Hoffstadt Bluffs Visitor Center, 146
Holiday Parade of Ships, 15
Hood, Mount, 8
Hood River, 128
Hospitals, 39
Howloween, 15
Hoyt Arboretum, 84–85
Huber's, 117
Hug Point State Recreation Site, 134

Imago Theatre, 113
Imbibe, 115–116
Insurance, 15–17
International Rose Test Garden, 7, 84, 86–87
Internet access, 22–23, 39
Irvington, 34
    accommodations, 52–53

Jack's Restaurant and Store, 148
Jake's Famous Crawfish, 117
Jamison Park, 103
Japanese Garden, 2, 84
The Japanese Garden, 87
Jazz, 115–116
Jeff Morris Memorial Fire Museum, 100
Jewelry, 110
Jimmy Mak's, 116
Johnston Ridge Observatory, 147

Kayaking, 7, 95
Keller Auditorium, 112–113
Kennedy School Theater, 124

Langlitz Leathers, 108
The Laura Russo Gallery, 105
Laurelhurst Theater, 124
Laurel Ridge Winery (Carlton), 141
Lava Canyon Trail, 149
Layout of Portland, 30
Leif Erikson Drive, 7–8, 93–94
Liquor laws, 39
The Lobby Court, 116

Lola's Room, 116
Lost-luggage insurance, 16–17
The Lucky Labrador Brew Pub, 121

McCormick and Schmick's Harbor-side Pilsner Room, 117–118
McMenamin's Kennedy School, 121
MacTarnahan's Tap Room, 120–121
Made in Oregon, 110
Main arteries and streets, 31
Manzanita, 134, 136
Maps, street, 32–33
Marathon, Portland, 15
Markets, 110
MAX (Metropolitan Area Express), 35–36
Medical insurance, 16
Meier and Frank, 108
Memorial Day Wine Tastings, 13
Metropolitan Area Express (MAX), 35–36
Mill Ends Park, 89
Mint/820, 117
Mio Gelato, 75
Mission Theater, 124
Money matters, 10–11
Moonstruck Chocolate Café, 73
Mother's Day Rhododendron Show, 13
Mount Hood Jazz Festival, 14
Mount Hood Meadows, 96
Mount Hood Railroad, 128, 130
Mt. Hood SkiBowl, 96
Mount St. Helens Cinedome Theater, 146
Mount St. Helens National Volcanic Monument, 144–149
Movie pubs, 124
Multnomah Falls, 125–126
Murdock Sky Theater, 82
Museum After Hours series, 114

Neahkahnie Mountain, 134
Nehalem Bay State Park, 135
Neighborhoods, in brief, 33–34
Newberg, 140
New Market Block, 101–102
Newmark Theater, 112
Newspapers and magazines, 39
New Theater Building, 112
Nightlife, 112–124
Nike Factory Company Store, 109
NIKETOWN Portland, 109

Nirvana Apothecary & Day Spa, 98
Nob Hill. *See* Northwest Portland
Noble Rot, 122
Noon Tunes, 14
Nordstrom, 108
Norm Thompson, 108
North and Northeast Portland
    brewpubs, 121
    restaurants, 69–70
Northern Oregon Coast, 132–139
The North Park Blocks, 102
Northwest Portland (including the
    Pearl District & Nob Hill), 34
    accommodations, 50–52
    brewpubs, 120–121
    restaurants, 63–67
    shopping, 104

Oaks Park, 9
Oaks Park Amusement Center, 90–91
¡Oba!, 118
Oceanside, 138
Oktoberfest, 14
The Old Church, 113
OMNIMAX theater, 82
Oneonta Gorge, 126
Opera, 114
Oregon Ballet Theatre, 113
Oregon Brewers Festival, 14
Oregon Historical Society Museum,
    80–81
Oregon Maritime Center and
    Museum, 82, 100
Oregon Museum of Science and
    Industry (OMSI), 8, 82
Oregon Symphony, 114
Oregon Wines on Broadway, 111,
    122–123
Oregon Zoo (Washington Park Zoo),
    3, 9, 14, 15, 87–88, 114
Organized tours, 91–93
Oswald West State Park, 134
Outdoor activities, 7–8, 93–97

Pacific City, 138
Parking, 37
Pastry shops, 74
Pearl Bakery, 74, 102
The Pearl District, 34, 83. *See also*
    Northwest Portland
    shopping, 104
    walking tour, 99–103

Peninsula Park Rose Garden, 89
Penner-Ash Wine Cellars (Yamhill),
    141
Performing arts, 112–115
Peter's Walking Tours of Portland, 92
Pharmacies, 39
Photographic needs, 39
Picnicking, 8
Pinot Station Tasting Room (Dundee),
    140
Pioneer Courthouse Square, 7, 77, 80,
    104
Pioneer Place, 110
Pittock Mansion, 88
Police, 39
Ponzi Wine Bar (Dundee), 140
Portland Art Museum, 81, 114
Portland Arts Festival, 13
Portland Audubon Society, 85
Portland Beavers Baseball Club,
    97–98
Portland Building, 80
Portland Center for the Performing
    Arts (PCPA), 112
Portland Center Stage, 114–115
Portland Children's Museum, 91
Portland City Grill, 119
Portland Classical Chinese Garden,
    83–84, 100
Portlandia, 80
Portland International Airport (PDX),
    28
    accommodations near, 54–56
Portland International Film Festival,
    13
Portland International Raceway, 97
Portland Marathon, 15
Portland Opera, 114
Portland Oregon Visitors Association
    (POVA), 10, 30, 32, 44, 140
Portland Outdoor Store, 108
The Portland Pendleton Shop,
    108–109
Portland River Company, 95, 97
Portland Rose Festival, 13
Portland Saturday Market, 7, 33, 84,
    100, 110
Portland Spirit, 91
Portland Streetcar, 36
Portland Tennis Center, 96
Portland Trail Blazers, 98
Portland Underground Tours, 93
Port of Cascade Locks Visitors Center,
    128

Post offices, 39–40
Powell's, 6
Powell's City of Books, 32, 103, 107
Pulliam Deffenbaugh Gallery, 106
Pumpkin Ridge Golf Club (North Plains), 94

Quintana Galleries, 102, 106

Rail travel, 27, 35–36, 92
  Mount Hood Railroad, 128, 130
Rain, average days of, 12
The Real Mother Goose, 107
Redtail Golf Course, 94
REI Co-Op, 95
Reptile and Amphibian Show, 14
The Reserve Vineyards and Golf Club (Hillsboro), 94
Restaurants, 57–75. *See also* Restaurants Index
  best, 5–6
  family-friendly, 69
  quick and cheap, 75
Restrooms, 40
Rex Hill Vineyards (Newberg), 140
Ringlers Pub, 116
River Drifters, 97
Rock music, 116
Rogue Ales Public House, 121
Roller skating, 9
Roots Brewing Co., 121
Rose City Golf Course, 94
Roseland Theater & Grill, 117
The Rose Quarter, 97
  accommodations, 52–53
Ross Island, 7

Safety, 40
Salon Nyla—The Day Spa, 98
Sand Castle Festival, 134
Saturday Market, 7, 33, 84, 100, 110
Saucebox, 119–120
Scandal's & The Otherside Lounge, 124
Scenic drives, Columbia Gorge, 2
Sea kayaking, 95
Seaside, 132
Seasons, 11–12
Sellwood/Westmoreland, 34
  antiques, 104–105

Seniors, 19–20
Shopping, 104–111
Sights and attractions, 76–93
  for kids, 90–91
  organized tours, 91–93
  suggested itineraries, 76–77
Skidmore Fountain, 101
Skidmore Historic District (Old Town), 33. *See also* Downtown
  walking tour, 99–103
Skiing, 8, 95–96
Smoking, 40
Sokol Blosser, 140
Southeast Portland
  brewpubs, 121
  restaurants, 70–73
Southpark Seafood Grill & Wine Bar, 123
Southwest Portland restaurants, 68
Special events and festivals, 13–15
Spectator sports, 97–98
Sportswear, 109
Staccato Gelato, 75
Star & Splendid, 105
Stars, 105
Street maps, 32–33
Stumptown Coffee Roasters, 73
Summer Concert Series, 14
Sunset Highway, 132
Sunset viewing, 6

The Tasting Room (Carlton), 141
Taxes, 40
Taxis, 37–38
Temperature, average, 12
Tennis, 96
Theater, 114–115
Three Capes Scenic Loop, 137
Ticketmaster, 113
Tickets West, 113
Tillamook, 137
Tillamook Cheese Factory, 137–138
Timberline Lodge, 130
Timberline Ski Area, 96
Time zone, 40
Tom McCall Waterfront Park. *See* Waterfront Park
Tours, organized, 91–93
Toys, 110
Train travel. *See* Rail travel
Transit info, 40
Transportation, 34–38

ACCOMMODATIONS INDEX **155**

Traveler's checks, 11
Travel insurance, 15–17
Trip-cancellation insurance, 15–16
Trolleys, vintage, 6–7, 35
Troutdale, accommodations, 54–56
Tryon Creek State Park, 95
Twist, 108
Tyrus Evan/The Depot (Carlton), 141

Union Station, 27, 30
Urban Wineworks, 122

Vancouver, Washington, accommo-
  dations, 53–54
Vault Martini, 120
Vietnam Veterans Living Memorial, 84
Vino Paradiso, 123
Vintage trolleys, 6–7, 35
Visitor information, 10
Vista House, 125

Walking tours
  guided, 92–93
  self-guided, 99–103
Washington Park, 84–89
Washington Park and Zoo Railway, 9,
  87
Washington Park Arboretum, 8
Washington Park Zoo. *See* Oregon
  Zoo
Waterfront Bicycle Rentals, 94
Waterfront Blues Festival, 14
Waterfront Park, 81, 90, 100
  summer festivals at, 3
Weather, 12
  information hot line, 40
Weather Machine, 80
White Bird, 113
White-water rafting, 97
Widmer Brewing and Gasthaus, 122
Willakenzie Estate (Yamhill), 141
Willamette Jetboat Excursions, 91–92
Willamette Shore Trolley, 92
Windy Ridge Viewpoint, 148
Wine bars, 122–123
Wine Country Thanksgiving, 15
Wine Down, 123
Wineries, 3, 93, 139
Wines, 111
Woods Creek Information Station,
  147

World Cup, 73
World Forestry Center Discovery
  Museum, 8, 88

Zoller's Outdoor Odysseys, 97
Zoo Lights, 15

ACCOMMODATIONS
Avalon Hotel & Spa, 3, 44
The Benson, 3, 48
Black Walnut Inn (Dundee), 141
Bonneville Hot Springs Resort (North
  Bonneville), 130–131
Coast Cabins (Manzanita), 136
Columbia Gorge Hotel (Hood River),
  131
Embassy Suites, 48–49, 51
Embassy Suites at Portland Airport,
  54–55
5th Avenue Suites Hotel, 3, 45
Four Points by Sheraton Portland
  Downtown, 4, 49
Governor Hotel, 45
The Heathman Hotel, 45–46
The Heathman Lodge (Vancouver,
  WA), 53
Heron Haus, 50
Homewood Suites by Hilton Vancou-
  ver/Portland (Vancouver, WA), 4, 51,
  54
Hotel Lucia, 46
Hotel Vintage Plaza, 4, 46–47
Inn at Cape Kiwanda (Pacific City),
  138–139
Inn @ Northrup Station, 4, 50
Jupiter Hotel, 4–5, 53
The Lakeshore Inn (Lake Oswego), 5,
  51, 56
The Lion and the Rose, 52
MacMaster House Bed and Breakfast
  Inn, 50–51
The Mark Spencer Hotel, 49
McMenamins Edgefield, 5, 55
McMenamins Grand Lodge (Forest
  Grove), 56
McMenamins Hotel Oregon (McMin-
  nville), 141–142
McMenamins Kennedy School, 5, 53
Portland Marriott Downtown Water-
  front, 47
Portland's White House, 52
RiverPlace Hotel, 4, 47–48

Silver Cloud Inn Portland Airport, 55–56
Silver Cloud Inn Portland Downtown, 51–52
Skamania Lodge (Stevenson), 131
Springbrook Hazelnut Farm (Newberg), 142
Stephanie Inn (Cannon Beach), 135
Timberline Lodge, 132
The Waves/The Argonauta Inn/White Heron Lodge (Cannon Beach), 135–136
Youngberg Hill Inn (McMinnville), 142–143

Restaurants

Assaggio, 71
Baan-Thai Restaurant, 62–63
Bijou Café, 5, 63, 69
Bistro Maison (McMinnville), 143
Bistro Restaurant (Cannon Beach), 136
Bluehour, 5, 63–64
Caffe Mingo, 65
Caprial's Bistro and Wine, 5, 70–71
Carafe Bistro, 60–61
Castagna, 71
Chart House, 5–6, 68
Currents (Nehalem), 137
Cuvée (Carlton), 143
Daily Café in the Pearl, 67
The Dundee Bistro, 143–144
Elephant's Deli, 67
Esparza's Tex-Mex Café, 72
Fong Chong, 63
Fratelli, 65–66
Genoa, 70
Good Dog/Bad Dog, 75
Gotham Building Tavern, 69
Gower Street Bistro (Cannon Beach), 136–137
The Heathman Restaurant and Bar, 57, 60
Higgins, 6, 60
Huber's, 6, 61
Jake's Famous Crawfish, 6, 61
The Joel Palmer House (Dayton), 144
Ken's Artisan Bakery, 74
Ken's Place, 71–72
McCormick and Schmick's Harborside at the Marina, 61–62
Newport Bay Restaurant, 6, 62, 69
Nicholas's, 72
Paley's Place, 64
Palio Dessert House, 74
Pambiche, 69–70
Papa Haydn West, 74
patanegra, 66
Peanut Butter & Ellie's, 68, 69
Pearl Bakery, 74, 102
Pelican Pub & Brewery (Pacific City), 139
Pho Van, 66
Piazza Italia, 66
Pix Patisserie, 74
Pizzicato Gourmet Pizza, 75
Rimsky-Korsakoffee House, 74
RingSide Downtown, 64
Salvador Molly's, 73
Southpark Seafood Grill & Wine Bar, 62
St. Honoré Boulangerie, 74
Tina's (Dundee), 144
Typhoon!, 60, 67
Veritable Quandary, 60
Wildwood, 64–65

FROMMER'S® DAY BY DAY GUIDES

Amsterdam	London	Rome
Chicago	New York City	San Francisco
Florence & Tuscany	Paris	Venice

FROMMER'S® NATIONAL PARK GUIDES

Algonquin Provincial Park	National Parks of the American West	Yosemite and Sequoia & Kings
Banff & Jasper	Rocky Mountain	Canyon
Grand Canyon	Yellowstone & Grand Teton	Zion & Bryce Canyon

FROMMER'S® MEMORABLE WALKS

Chicago	New York	Rome
London	Paris	San Francisco

FROMMER'S® WITH KIDS GUIDES

Chicago	National Parks	Toronto
Hawaii	New York City	Walt Disney World® & Orlando
Las Vegas	San Francisco	Washington, D.C.
London		

SUZY GERSHMAN'S BORN TO SHOP GUIDES

Born to Shop: France	Born to Shop: Italy	Born to Shop: New York
Born to Shop: Hong Kong, Shanghai	Born to Shop: London	Born to Shop: Paris
& Beijing		

FROMMER'S® IRREVERENT GUIDES

Amsterdam	Los Angeles	Rome
Boston	Manhattan	San Francisco
Chicago	New Orleans	Walt Disney World®
Las Vegas	Paris	Washington, D.C.
London		

FROMMER'S® BEST-LOVED DRIVING TOURS

Austria	Germany	Northern Italy
Britain	Ireland	Scotland
California	Italy	Spain
France	New England	Tuscany & Umbria

THE UNOFFICIAL GUIDES®

Adventure Travel in Alaska	Hawaii	Paris
Beyond Disney	Ireland	San Francisco
California with Kids	Las Vegas	South Florida including Miami &
Central Italy	London	the Keys
Chicago	Maui	Walt Disney World®
Cruises	Mexico's Best Beach Resorts	Walt Disney World® for
Disneyland®	Mini Las Vegas	Grown-ups
England	Mini Mickey	Walt Disney World® with Kids
Florida	New Orleans	Washington, D.C.
Florida with Kids	New York City	

SPECIAL-INTEREST TITLES

Athens Past & Present	Frommer's Exploring America by RV
Cities Ranked & Rated	Frommer's NYC Free & Dirt Cheap
Frommer's Best Day Trips from London	Frommer's Road Atlas Europe
Frommer's Best RV & Tent Campgrounds	Frommer's Road Atlas Ireland
in the U.S.A.	Retirement Places Rated

FROMMER'S® PHRASEFINDER DICTIONARY GUIDES

French	Italian	Spanish

THE NEW TRAVELOCITY GUARANTEE

EVERYTHING YOU BOOK WILL BE RIGHT, OR WE'LL WORK WITH OUR TRAVEL PARTNERS TO MAKE IT RIGHT, RIGHT AWAY.

To drive home the point,
we're going to use the word "right" in every single sentence.

Let's get right to it. Right to the meat! Only Travelocity guarantees everything about your booking will be right, or we'll work with our travel partners to make it right, right away. Right on!

Here's a picture taken smack dab right in the middle of Antigua, where the guarantee also covers you.

The guarantee covers all but one of the items pictured to the right.

For example, what if the ocean view you booked actually looks out at a downright ugly parking lot? You'd be right to call – we're there for you. And no one in their right mind would be pleased to learn the rental car place has closed and left them stranded. Call Travelocity and we'll help get you back on the right track.

Now, you may be thinking, "Yeah, right, I'm so sure." That's OK; you have the right to remain skeptical. That is until we mention help is always right around the corner. Call us right off the bat, knowing that our customer service reps are there for you 24/7. Righting wrongs. Left and right.

Now if you're guessing there are some things we can't control, like the weather, well you're right. But we can help you with most things – to get all the details in righting,* visit **travelocity.com/guarantee**.

*Sorry, spelling things right is one of the few things not covered under the guarantee.

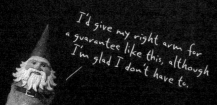

I'd give my right arm for a guarantee like this, although I'm glad I don't have to.

travelocity
You'll never roam alone.

IF YOU BOOK IT, IT SHOULD BE THERE.

Only Travelocity guarantees it will be, or we'll work with our travel partners to make it right, right away. So if you're missing a balcony or anything else you booked, just call us 24/7. **1-888-TRAVELOCITY.**

travelocit
You'll never roam al